The people's book

A history of Williamson Park Lancaster

SUZANNE BRADSHAW

By the same author
The Forgotten Keepers of the Judges' Lodgings, which tells about the hidden lives of the
servants who looked after the Lodgings and the judges when they were in residence
https://lancasterjudgeslodgings.org.uk/new-book-launch/

First published in 2022
by Palatine Books,
Carnegie House,
Chatsworth Road
Lancaster LA1 4SL
www.palatinebooks.com

British Library Cataloguing-in-Publication data
A catalogue record for this book is available from the British Library

Every effort has been made to trace copyright holders. Some of the images used in this publication are
orphaned images from the collections at Lancaster City Museums. If you are the creator or rights holder of
any of these images, please do get in touch.

Paperback ISBN 13: 978-1-910837-39-9

Designed and typeset by Carnegie Book Production
www.carnegiebookproduction.com

Printed and bound by Cambrian Printers

Contents

Acknowledgements

I would like to thank the following people and organisations for their contributions and support to this project:

Lancashire Archives, Preston; Red Rose Collections; Community History Section, Lancaster Library; Sue Ashworth; the Friends of Williamson Park; Lancaster City Museum; Kendal Museum; and, last but not least, members of Lancaster and District Heritage Group for their encouragement and support.

This book was researched and produced by Sue Bradshaw. Thanks are due to Nigel Neil and Gary Bradshaw for their suggestions and assistance. Finally, thanks to Anna and Lucy at Carnegie Publishing for embracing this project and helping me fulfil my ambition to get the park's history into print.

Foreword

Like so many of the residents of Lancaster, I cherish Williamson Park, whether on sunny summer days or in the bleakest of windy winters.

On one visit to the park in 2018 I decided I wanted to know more about it, so I went to buy a book on its history. I was disappointed to discover that no such book existed, however. My initial surprise and disappointment soon changed to resolve: 'If no such book exists, then I will write one!'

I realised that although I have walked around the park hundreds of times over the past decades, I actually knew very little about it, and presumably I was not the only one. I began with a vague idea that it would be good to do a brief general 'biography' of the park, and set off in search of the story. In gathering facts about the site of the park I began to appreciate that it is as much about people as it is about buildings and landscapes. I realised that I was not only discovering the facts of how the park came into being, but also encountering people. I found characters whose lives had influenced the development of Williamson Park, people whose names and efforts have largely been forgotten. I knew that I wanted these men and women to accompany me on my walk through the history of the park.

It has been a fascinating journey for me, and now when I walk along the paths and through the dells of our great local park I can see it as it was at different stages in its past. I can imagine it as a place inhabited by Bronze Age 'Lancastrians' solemnly burying the urns containing their dead on the bleak gorse-covered hilltop. I can imagine the suffering of the poor souls whose lives ended brutally on Gallows Hill, and the impoverished unemployed mill workers building the road during the cotton famine. I can imagine the noise and commotion of the working quarries and the men loading stone onto their carts, ready to take it down the hill to build Lancaster. And I can imagine the workers building the Memorial, and tending to the gardens during the two world wars.

A walk through the park can be a vivid act of imagination and appreciation. It is my hope that others will be able to use this book to enhance their experience of the park, but most of all I hope that people will enjoy this beautiful place.

One of the gardeners' lodges

Introduction

The history of Williamson Park is the history of Lancaster's people, both poor and wealthy, from the out-of-work mill hands to the Victorian philanthropists. The park was laid out on land known as Lancaster Moor, an area of common land where local townsfolk would take their cattle to graze, and quarrymen worked to obtain a source of good sandstone to provide building materials for the fine Georgian buildings still standing in Lancaster today.

Much earlier than that, in the Bronze Age, the Moor was used as a burial place for funerary urns, one of which can still be seen in Lancaster Museum.

It also has a sinister side to its history, being a place of execution, and was known as Gallows Hill or Tyburn on the Moor. Roman Catholic martyrs, Pendle witches and various malefactors or wrongdoers were tried at Lancaster Castle and brought to the site to meet their end. For many years the area was a source of good sandstone and the quarry walls are still very much in evidence in the landscaping of the park today. The beautiful scenery we enjoy was once a busy and noisy place of work for quarrymen over many years.

DID YOU KNOW?

The Bronze Age in Britain started around 2500 BCE and ended roughly 800 BCE when the Iron Age began.

The beginnings of the park as we now know it took shape during the Cotton Famine of the early 1860s. The land began to be developed under the Poor Law Act, with the construction of roads over the Moor, work which gave

The 'sliding rock' area at the end of the lake

paid employment to out-of-work cotton mill workers and saved them from possible starvation. It was only after this period of initial development that serious plans were implemented in the late 1870s by James Williamson and, after his death, his son, Lord Ashton, to give to the people of Lancaster a place of relaxation and recreation, the 'lung of Lancaster' which became known as Williamson Park.

For all of its history, of course, the site of the park has been a perfect vantage

The top path alongside the Friends of Williamson Park garden area

point from which to view the stunning surrounding landscape – from the Lakeland fells to the north, Morecambe Bay to the west, the Bowland fells to the east and the Fylde coast to the south.

In this book I will be charting the stages of the park's evolution and looking at the characters who contributed towards its creation and its maintenance.

Quernmore Road

Wyresdale Road

1 Pavilion Café
2 Shop
3 Butterfly House
4 Ashton Memorial
5 Mini Beasts
6 Bird Enclosure
7 Sun Dial
8 Temple Shelter
9 Waterfall
10 The Dell
11 Fenham Carr Woodland Walk
12 Greg Observatory Site
13 Playground
14 Reservoir (no access)
15 Raku Sculpture
16 Toilets
   Cycle Path (marked in orange)

Plan of the park showing all the main features

The Bronze Age

On the high ridge of land running from Lancaster Cemetery, across Williamson Park, through Golgotha, and then on to the former Bowerham Barracks site (an area now covered by part of the University of Cumbria), have been found a significant number of Bronze Age burials. The settlement sites which would have been associated with these burials have not yet been found, but it is likely they lay in the surrounding land (*Desktop Archaeological Assessment,* 22 November 2017, Lancashire Archaeological Advisory Service).

Dr Harker and the Lancaster Moor burial urns

Dr John Harker was a local physician and surgeon living at 11 King Street in Lancaster, but he also had an interest in history and archaeology, as he was one of the curators at Lancaster Museum (the other being a Dr Moore). This work was probably carried out in his spare time, as it is never listed as his occupation on the census returns. By 1891 he had risen to be a Justice of the Peace and was then living at Hazel Grove in Yealand Redmayne, as well as still being listed as a physician and surgeon. He later became a County Magistrate. He died in 1904, aged 70, his obituary stating that he had been a president of Royal Lancaster Infirmary, was Lancaster's Medical Officer for 17 years, and ex-president of the Lancashire Branch of the British Medical Association.

In 1864, during the working of the land on the Moor as quarries, six distinct Bronze Age burial urns were found. The location was 'a little to the south of the most elevated part of the people's recreation ground' (*Lancaster Observer* 29 October 1864) in land being quarried by men

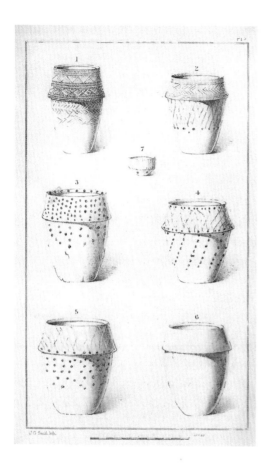

Urns from Lancaster Moor, *Journal of the British Archaeological Association* (*JBAA*), 1865, Harker.

employed by a Mr Harrison (see section on Lancaster Moor's quarrymen).

The urns eventually came into the possession of Dr Harker. He submitted details of the finds on Lancaster Moor in an article for the *British Journal of Archaeology*, stating that the urns were found about eight feet down, the top six feet consisting of broken stone from the quarry. They were found 'in pairs, at intervals of a yard, in a long line extending east and west'. He described the land to the east of the site of the burial of these urns as consisting of barrows (large mounds of earth, often covering burials), and at the eastern extremity the land 'inclines steeply towards the Asylum ground'. The urns in this area were 'so much decayed ... as scarcely to be recognisable' (*Journal of the British Archaeological Association*, 1865).

Urns 1 and 2 in the illustration were found side-by-side, 'a thick flag nearly two feet square between them, and another heavy flag resting on the uprights, so as to cover the mouths of both vessels'. Urn 1 contained an unburnt bone from the head of a fish and a bronze 'blade of an arrow or dart with a rivet hole in its broad tang'. The companion urn, number 2, is stated to have contained the bones of a female, so perhaps these cremations represented a couple.

The rest of the urns were found upright, their mouths simply covered with pieces of flag. Urn number 3 had no associated grave goods and is currently on display in Lancaster City Museum. The plain urn, number 6 in the illustration, contained 'the bones of a muscular man in larger fragments than those found in the other vessels'. It also contained a bone of an uncertain animal and portions of pins made of deer horn. Two of the pieces were perforated, perhaps to allow them to be hung from a garment.

The small item, number 7 in the illustration, was thought by Harker to be an incense cup at the time, but these are now usually described as funerary cups, as their exact function is uncertain. He does not specify which urn this was associated with, but described it as being 3 inches in diameter with two holes on one side of its lower part and made of fine clay. This cup is also currently on display in Lancaster City Museum.

Harker described the portions of bones found as being of a small type, 'the portions of the skulls being fine and thin. They are calcined, in small fragments, and with them are mingled ashes and little stones', and he comments that it was remarkable that he had not found any teeth.

In a letter to the *Lancaster Observer* (29 October 1864) Harker stated that 'portions of a curious flattened copper ornament still remain in the hands of the work people'. His paper in the journal explains that it was deliberately broken up by the workmen, as they thought it was gold and wanted to share it between them! This would be the item bottom left

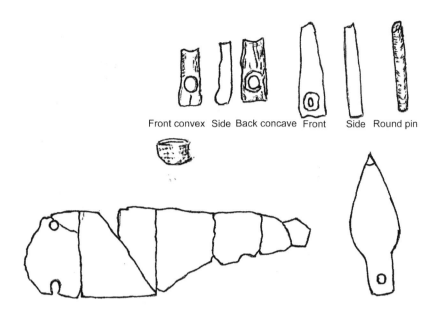

Front convex Side Back concave Front   Side Round pin

in the illustration above. The deer pins are at the top and the knife blade is bottom right.

Eight years later, in 1872, Dr Harker wrote about the discovery of a further complete urn on Lancaster Moor in the same locality as the previous finds and on the same line of direction (Longworth also states that this urn is lost). It was again discovered by quarrymen, who unfortunately broke it in their haste to uncover it. It was inverted rather than upright, and surrounded by 'board, charcoal and ashes, the relics of the funeral pyre'. Although there is no illustration, it is well-described as being decorated with lines made by indenting strips of fine twisted thong, and dots formed by the use of a stick. There were no associated burial goods, but the pot contained well-calcined human bones. He stated that the 'upper and lower jaw were both carefully sought for and examined. The teeth had been removed from their alveoli [sockets], and taken away'. He speculated that the teeth from this burial and the previous ones may have been deliberately removed from the jaws to 'adorn the persons of the living', as practised by other civilisations. In his paper published in the *Journal of the British Archaeological Association*, it is of interest that Dr Harker mentioned that fragments of other urns had been brought to him by the 'workpeople' on the Moor, showing the extent and large number of the interments.

Dr Harker also notes that a further 'small incense vessel' was also found in the same locality as this urn and he described it as being more globose in form than the example in the previous diagram, and the details of its ornamentation are described as 'pleasing'. This cup is also currently on display in Lancaster City Museum.

Lancaster Museum was at that time housed in the Mechanics' Institute (now known as The Storey), and Dr Harker agreed to put together the fragments of the urns found at Lancaster Moor and to lodge them in the Museum (*Lancaster Gazette* 10 December 1864). He later acquired the missing portions of metal from the quarrymen, which formed a 'triangular British knife blade' and also two more 'deer horn pins'. Dr Harker handed all the finds over to Lancaster Corporation, who agreed the grand sum of £5 to provide a display case for the finds to be placed in the museum.

The Bowerham Barracks urns

Another four years later, in 1876, a further group of urns was found (*Lancaster Guardian* 20 December 1876) during the building of Bowerham Barracks, at the top of Coulston Road, on land now owned by the University of Cumbria. Harker states that the urns were found at the highest part of the military estate and that there were 'about 300 yards' between this discovery and the Lancaster Moor urns.

There were six urns, grouped in pairs in a line from east to west, just as with the Moor urns, which were simply buried a few inches below ground level. Unfortunately, the workmen broke up all but one specimen which was found within an urn of 'much larger size, over which was a coverlet or lid something like the size and shape of a cardinal's hat'. The interior urn was around eight inches in height (see illustration overleaf) and filled with calcined bones. The exterior urn is described as being of a coarser structure and looking something like urn number 3 in the previous illustration. Harker then states that 'This pot [presumably the larger one] was filled with calcined bones, and in it was found an extremely pretty limestone ornament, 4 inches broad, convex in front, and smooth at the back. At each end is a very fine perforation'. The stone was unburnt and highly polished, a 'mountain limestone … very dark and bright

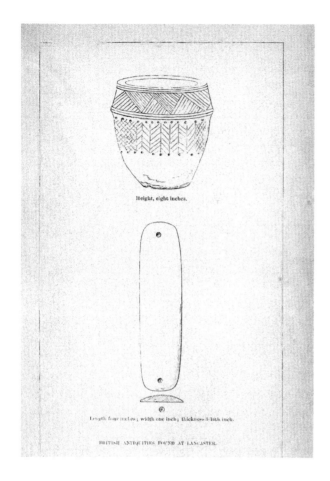

Height, eight inches.

Length four inches; width one inch; thickness 3/10th inch.

BRITISH ANTIQUITIES FOUND AT LANCASTER.

in appearance'. This stone is described by Longworth as being an archer's wrist guard.

Mr Harker had examined the bones, particularly the jaw bones, and found that again the teeth had been removed from their alveoli, like the Lancaster Moor finds, and he similarly speculated that they had been deliberately removed as 'keepsakes to adorne the persons of the living'.

The smaller urn is currently on display in Lancaster Museum, together with the wrist guard.

Burial urn from Lancaster Cemetery

The final urn was found in 1894 by a labourer called Hartley when digging (presumably a grave) on 'nearly the highest portion of the cemetery, in open space east of the Crimean Monument' (correspondence column, *Lancaster Guardian* 9 June 1894). It was lying only four inches below the surface and the upper half was smashed due to the labourer not having seen it immediately. The cemetery registrar, Mr John Barton, who lived in the cemetery lodge on Quernmore Road, gathered up all the pieces and showed them to the anonymous letter writer (possibly Dr Harker), who estimated the size to be 13.5 inches in height, 10 inches in diameter, tapering to 5 inches at the bottom. There is no illustration of this urn, but the decoration was described as being plain on the lower half, the upper half having 'four slightly indented rings made when on the potter's wheel, and a small raised ring just under the neck; between the third and fourth rings there was a cross or check pattern marking'. The contents were 'fragments of bone … mixed with dry earth, but no metal'. There is no record of this urn in Longworth's *Collared Urns* and it is not known what was done with the fragments.

As mentioned previously, one of the urns and the two small cups found on the Moor and also the urn from Bowerham Barracks can be seen in the Museum today, but the other items have sadly been lost.

The discovery of many urns and of two funerary cups spread over such a large area on this site high above the city of Lancaster show that this was a significant Bronze Age site. Dr Harker commented about their use of this elevated site, with its far-reaching views, as a cemetery: 'The choice of this site by an ancient tribe shows human appreciation of the grand and poetic in the selection of a last resting-place for the bones of the honoured dead.'

Gallows Hill

For centuries the site of Lancaster Moor was a place of execution. Many unfortunate souls found guilty of crimes at Lancaster Castle's Court were hanged on the moor at Gallows Hill, also known as Tyburn on the Moor.

A plan of Lancaster from 1684 (compiled by Kenneth Docton from a map discovered in Towneley Hall, Burnley, in 1954) shows the distance to 'Tiburn' as 574 yards (around 525 metres) from the bottom of Moor Lane would take us just above the junction of Park Road and Moor Gate, approximately where the triangular Park Square now stands.

Yates' 1786 map of Lancashire marks the site of the gallows as being below the site of the quarries on the Moor, but above the fork in the roads leading to Quernmore in the north and Abbeystead in the south. Although its exact site is not known for certain, this places it very close to the area in which the park now stands. Peel and Southern's book, *The trials of the Lancashire Witches*, claims that the place of execution was 'about a mile from the castle on a site now overbuilt by an extension to Lancaster

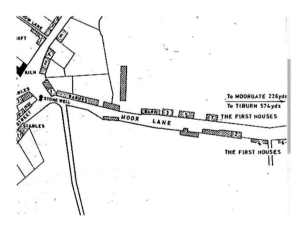

Section of 1684 plan of Lancaster by Docton, showing distance to 'Tiburn'

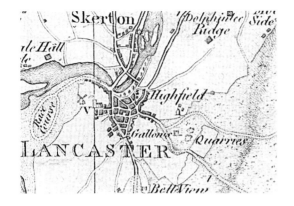

Section of 1786 map of Lancashire by Yates, showing site of gallows

DID YOU KNOW?

The name Tyburn was synonymous with capital punishment, it having been the principal place in London for execution of criminals and convicted traitors, including many religious martyrs.

Royal Grammar School'. This would place the gallows to the eastern side of Wyresdale Road, roughly opposite to Christ Church.

Martyrs and Witches

Between the years 1584 and 1646, at least fifteen Roman Catholic martyrs were put to death by being hanged, drawn and quartered at Gallows Hill, according to the harsh regime persecuting Catholics which began in the English Reformation. It was seen as an act of treason punishable by death to be a Roman Catholic priest, or to assist or harbour a priest.

In 1628, one such priest, Edmund Arrowsmith, was found guilty of 'taking the order of priesthood contrary to the laws of the realm'. He was bound to a hurdle fastened to a horse and was dragged through the streets to the gallows at Tyburn on the Moor. While on the gallows he was urged by a magistrate to repent. When he refused to do so, he was cast off the ladder, then hanged and quartered in front of a great

Portrait of Edmund Arrowsmith

Drawing based on seventeenth-century woodcuts showing witches hanging

crowd, before his head was placed on a spike on the battlements of the Castle's Gateway Tower (Dan Sailor, *The County Hanging Town*).

Perhaps better known are the events surrounding the Pendle witches who were tried and executed at Lancaster in August 1612. Out of 19 people accused of witchcraft in Lancashire at that time, nine were hanged at Gallows Hill, the day after their trial at Lancaster Castle. Much has already been written elsewhere about this infamous episode in Lancaster's history, and many books have based their accounts on Thomas Potts' *The Wonderfull Discoverie of Witches in the Countie of Lancaster*. Potts was Clerk to the Court but his account, the only record from the time, was not a verbatim transcribing of the trial. It was written some months after the trial and cannot entirely be relied upon as being completely accurate, as it was commissioned and edited by the trial judges, with an eye to their reputations and careers. Nevertheless, there is much in Potts' book that contributes to our knowledge.

The mystery of Alice Nutter: Witch or Catholic?

Alice Nutter is one of the lesser-known Pendle Witches who was tried and hanged along with the others in 1612. She did not quite fit with the others accused, who were poverty-stricken and ill-educated, as she was of a higher social standing. Thomas Potts described her as 'having a fine dwelling, a rich woman blessed with great estate, had good reputation, good temper and free from malice'. The only accusation against her was that she had been present at a witches' 'sabbat' meeting at Malkin Tower, the home of 'Old Demdike', on Good Friday. During the trial she spoke little and was refused the possibility of calling witnesses in her defence, though she maintained her innocence.

It has been suggested that the explanation for her keeping quiet during the trial was that she may have been a Catholic (catholicherald.co.uk/ issues/oct-5th-2018/alice-nutter-a-witch-or-a-secret-catholic). She could therefore not reveal her whereabouts on Good Friday if she had been at a Mass and did not want to implicate others who were taking part in what was an illegal activity. Another link to the Catholic faith is that two of the Catholic martyrs were also named Nutter and from the Pendle area; John Nutter was executed at Tyburn in 1584 and his brother, Robert Nutter, at Lancaster in 1600, only twelve years before Alice.

Between the years 1782 and 1799 at least 47 hangings took place at Gallows Hill for crimes ranging from murder and highway robbery to horse stealing and theft from bleaching grounds (bleaching grounds were

Illustration from *Lancashire Stories* by Frank Hird – execution at Gallows Hill

EXECUTION AT GALLOWS HILL

found in and around mill towns and were an open area used for spreading cloth on the ground to be purified and whitened by the action of the sun).

The illustration above shows condemned prisoners being transported up to Gallows Hill in a springless cart with their backs to the horses, their coffins piled up behind them. Frank Hird (*Lancashire Stories, c.*1900) states that as many as eight or nine prisoners would be hanged at the same time: 'The doleful procession passed along Moor Lane and Moor Gate, stopping at the Golden Lion public house in order that the condemned might take their last drink.'

The tale of Mary Hilton, condemned to death for poisoning her husband

Frank Hird also tells the horrendous story of Mary Hilton, who was executed in 1772 after being tried for petty treason and found guilty at Lancaster Assizes of poisoning her husband. She was drawn on a sledge to the gallows and, after hanging for 15 minutes, she was cut down and her body burned. He recorded that

> An old inhabitant of Lancaster, whose recollections were taken down early in the nineteenth century, said that Mary Hilton, who lived at Four Lane Ends, was burned opposite the second window of the workhouse. She was first strangled by a man with one arm, and before she was dead was let down into a fire consisting of faggots and two barrels of tar. She was beginning to move before the fire reached her.

DID YOU KNOW?

Petty or Petit Treason was defined by the Treason Act of 1351 and encompassed the killing of a master by a servant or a husband by his wife.

It was only after 1800 that hangings took place at the Castle, when the Crown Court was completed, the last execution at Lancaster Moor taking place on 27 April 1799.

Lancaster Moor's quarrymen

The quarries in the nineteenth century

There were several quarries on Lancaster Moor, most leased by the Corporation to various stonemasons or quarrymen. The income from renting out the land on the Moor was £40 in 1861 and rose to nearly double that in 1874, at £78 16s. 1d., and again to £102 0s. 6d. in 1877, the year in which James Williamson senior first offered to fund the creation of a pleasure ground on the Moor. The quarries provided good quality sandstone for the rebuilding of Lancaster in the eighteenth century, during Lancaster's 'golden age', and there were up to seven separate quarries on the Moor at this time (Andrew White, *The Buildings of Georgian Lancaster*).

Some plans of the quarries on the Moor dating from the early nineteenth century show up to ten quarries, some with the name of the tenant, so it is clear that the tenancies of quarries on the Moor changed over time.

The 1820 plan shows the buildings of the workhouse in the bottom-right corner and the asylum in the top left, although these are not labelled. The quarry marked as 'Poor House Quarry' was likely to have been where some of the male inmates were put to work quarrying; stone-breaking being a common form of work given to men who were resident in workhouses. The workhouse itself had been built in 1788 on the south side of Quernmore Road, adjacent to the site of the quarries.

DID YOU KNOW?

A poor house is another term for a workhouse.

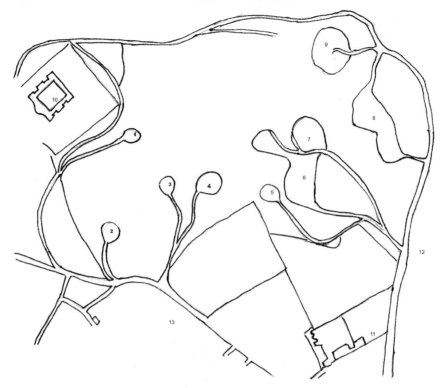

Index to 1820 plan of quarries

1. Corporation Quarry
2. Poor House Quarry
3. Bell's Quarry
4. Lowther's Quarry
5. Late Holmes Quarry
6. Late Taylor, now Lowther's Quarry
7. Howson's Quarry
8. Bell Company Quarry
9. County Quarry
10. Asylum
11. Workhouse
12. Road to Clitheroe
13. Road to Asylum

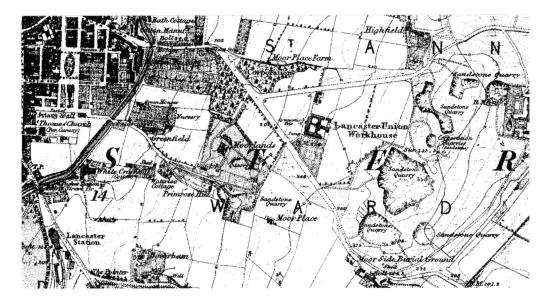

1845 six-inch Ordnance Survey map

The 1845 six-inch ordnance survey map shows seven quarries still being worked on the Moor lying to the east of the workhouse building, and you can also see the tracks leading to them which enabled the quarried stone to be easily removed.

It seems the Corporation was often unhappy with the way in which various tenants worked their quarries. In 1863, during initial plans to convert the Moor into a park, Mr Thomas Storey, a prominent citizen of Lancaster and co-founder of Storey Brothers factory, expressed concerns about how the quarries were being worked:

DID YOU KNOW?

Storey Brothers factory was founded in 1849 and manufactured leathercloth and table baize. Thomas was four times mayor of Lancaster, and received the honour of knighthood in 1887. He was very benevolent, and took a great interest in local institutions. He provided the funding for the building of the Storey Institute which was renamed after him in his honour in 1891. Its purpose was for 'the promotion of art, science, literature, and technical instruction' (https://www.lancaster.gov.uk/sites/the-storey/about-the-storey).

Lancaster from the Stone Quarries (detail), c.1870, William Linton (Lancaster City Museums LANLM.1998.17)

> At present anyone that took them could pick here and pick there, until the place presented the appearance of a lot of pigs rooting up the ground.

At that time the quarries were only being let from month to month so that 'they [the corporation] would not be inconvenienced at any time they wanted the place' (*Lancaster Guardian* 31 October 1863). They were obviously already thinking about enclosing the land at this point.

We meet some of the quarrymen: Thomas Harrison, Edward Gorrill and the Taylor family

Thomas Harrison was one of the main quarrymen renting a quarry on the Moor (see A tale of rags to riches in two generations p 24). In the 1871 census he was a master mason employing 68 men and boys, and he lived in close proximity to the Moor at 48 Moor Lane.

Two of his sons were also employed as stonemasons. In 1868 Mr Harrison rented the South Quarry from the Corporation for five years at a cost of £21 per year. The contract only allowed him to employ a maximum of ten men including labourers (*Committee Minute Books*, Lancashire Archives). In 1874 the Moor sub-committee of the Corporation asked the surveyor to draw up a new contract with Mr Harrison with regard to his working of the South Quarry and one of its provisions was that 'the Surveyor confine Mr Harrison's working to such places as shall be approved' (*Lancaster Guardian*, 22 August 1874).

Another quarryman, Mr Edward Gorrill, lived next to the Moor Quarries at the 94-acre Stoney Head Farm. In 1874 he was told by the Corporation in no uncertain terms that he was working the North Quarry in an 'injurious' manner and that 'proceedings would be taken for his unauthorised working' of the same. A couple of months later it was reported by the Town Clerk that Mr Gorrill had now ceased working this quarry and it had now been re-let (*Lancaster Guardian* 22 August 1874, 26 September 1874).

The following year the Corporation was taking a much firmer stance with those who were letting quarries from them, as the contracts drawn up that year were to be 'subject to stringent powers in case of breach of term' (*Lancaster Gazette* 24 April 1875).

It is also evident that people were in the habit of using the Moor as a source of materials other than for quarrying stone, as the Committee Minute Books reveal in 1870: 'Information was laid before the Committee that Workmen and others employed by the Phoenix Foundry were in the habit of getting sand loam and soil from or otherwise trespassing on the Moor'. It was resolved that the Town Clerk would write to the Foundry on the subject.

The stone quarries were still providing work for many Lancaster men well into the nineteenth century. The 1851 census counted 42 men whose occupation was listed as 'Quarryman', but 144 as either stonemason, stonemason's apprentice,

DID YOU KNOW?

The Phoenix Foundry was situated on Phoenix Street. In 1852 Edmund Sharpe, architect, became the proprietor of the Phoenix Foundry, which among other things supplied cast iron pipes for the Lancaster waterworks, sewers and drains, and shells for the Crimean War.

stonemason's labourer or stonemason journeyman. Many of the men working as stonemasons created family businesses by employing their sons, first as apprentices and then as stonemasons. This created a situation where stonemasonry as an occupation was passed down through the generations.

An example of this is the Taylor family. In 1851 Thomas Taylor was listed as a stonemason employing 3 men – two of these were his sons, Thomas junior and John, who were listed as stonemason's apprentices. Ten years later Thomas senior was doing very well and had expanded his business to employ 14 men and 2 boys. He had clearly moved up in the world as his address had changed from Upper Thurnham Street, a street of tiny terraced houses, to Springfield Terrace, a newer and more upmarket property. Thomas junior was now a fully-fledged stonemason and had set up home with his wife Ann on Upper King Street. Thomas junior then diversified into being a 'letter cutter' in addition to carrying on as a stonemason – this meant he was skilled in cutting letters into stone, for such items as headstones, house names or architectural lettering. By 1881 Thomas junior had now become a marble mason and letter cutter, so had specialised into working with marble, possibly just carrying out work on headstones. His 22-year-old son, Edward, was also employed as a marble mason and letter cutter, meaning that by now the craft of stonemasonry had been passed down through at least three generations.

A tale of rags to riches in two generations: the Harrison dynasty

In 1841 two brothers, Thomas and Henry Harrison, aged 23 and 21, both stonemasons, lived on a tiny back street, coincidentally named Mason Street, which was really just a back alley positioned in between North Road and St Leonardgate. Thomas's wife, Agnes, aged 22, also lived with them. The living conditions would have been very poor, as would many others in the centre of Lancaster at that time. Indeed, Dr Richard Owen, Lancaster's famous son who coined the word 'dinosaur' and who was also superintendent of the natural history department of the British Museum, described the poverty and its impact on the inhabitants of Lancaster in his 1845 *Report on the state of Lancaster* for the Health of Towns Commission. In particular he described Mason Street as follows:

… the Medical Officer had found the stench of this place so intolerable as to be compelled to quit his patient as soon as possible … The degree of domestic cleanliness with these evils to contend against were, notwithstanding, highly creditable to the poor women, the wives of the operatives who tenant these abodes. But too frequently, the effect of the difficulties and constant operation of surrounding annoyances … was manifest in the sordid, sickly and querulous slatterns, into which women of originally cleanly and orderly habits had sunk, combining to render the interior of their abodes as intolerable to the husband and children as the exterior was disgusting.

By the time of the 1851 census the brothers had set up home separately, Thomas at 1 Moor Place on Moor Lane, and Henry with his wife Margaret at Bath Mill Cottages. Thomas was still working as a stonemason, but brother Henry was doing remarkably well and was a stonemason employing 27 men. It was around this time that the Harrison brothers set up a co-operative with Robert Wilson, a joiner and builder, and Robert Grisdale, a plasterer, to build a terrace of houses on St George's Quay (numbers 1 to 11) (*Victorian Terraced Houses in Lancaster*, Andrew White and Michael Winstanley). They took equal shares in the land and materials, and also in the finished houses. It was normal practice for the stonemasons to put up the shell of the building, with the other trades completing the project.

By 1861 Thomas seems to have taken over the Harrison building firm, as he was then recorded as being a master builder employing 35 men, perhaps because Henry was shown as the Borough Surveyor, an important role in Lancaster Borough Council. He had been selected for this position in 1858 against considerable competition, after 'applications and testimonials of several candidates, 13 in number, were placed before the board and duly considered' (*Lancaster Guardian* 11 December 1858). Thomas's 18-year-old son was employed as a stonemason's apprentice and was made a freeman of Lancaster at this young age (*Lancaster Guardian* 3 August 1861). The two families seemed to be sharing number 107 Moor Lane, although it must have been a large house, probably split into two, as Thomas had eight children and Henry had four, in addition to his mother-in-law living with them!

Mason Street in 1914 (Courtesy of Lancashire County Council's Red Rose Collections)

Henry Harrison died in 1869 aged just 49, and his widow Margaret is listed as living on 'houses and dividends' at 49 Moor Lane with her now six children in the 1871 census. Henry and Margaret's sons went on to occupations outside stonemasonry and building, Thomas becoming a pawnbroker at 28 Market Street, and William a commercial traveller. Henry's brother Thomas was now listed as a master mason employing 68 men and eight boys and was living at 48 Moor Lane, next door to his widowed sister-in-law. It is possible that the houses on Moor Lane had been renumbered in the intervening years since 1861. Thomas rented the South Quarry on the Moor from the Corporation (*Lancaster Guardian* 22 August 1874). Thomas's two sons, Henry and William, were also working as stonemasons in 1871, and they both carried on the stonemason family tradition after Thomas's death in 1879, but with very different outcomes.

By the time of the next census in1881, Henry was an unemployed stonemason living on Rosemary Lane, which would have been very poor housing, while his brother William had taken over their father's business as a master builder, employing 66 men and six boys, and was living at 49 Moor Lane, which was previously the home of his borough-surveyor uncle, his widow Margaret also having died. It seems that William did not provide work for his brother, so it is likely that Henry was ill and unable to work. Indeed, by 1891 Henry is listed as a 'retired stonemason' but is only aged 47, which adds weight to this theory. He died at the age of 50, living on De Vitre Street. It is possible that the more successful William provided in some way for his brother.

Meanwhile, William had become a very successful builder. In 1886 he built Cumberland View, just off Bowerham Road. In 1888 he built the north side of Havelock Street, also in Bowerham, and added three further houses in 1891. He is also known to have built some of the houses on Clarence Street in the Primrose area in 1901–2. By this time the quarries on the Moor had been closed and the land converted into the park, but William now owned a quarry on Primrose Hill, known as 'Scotch Quarry' and also now converted into a public green space. This quarry was very conveniently placed for building projects in both Bowerham and Primrose.

Around 1897 the Harrison building firm was employed by Peter Paul Pugin, the son of the famous architect Augustus Pugin, to build a house in Skerton for Miss Margaret Coulston, the house today being the Presbytery for St Joseph's Church on Slyne Road (stjosephslancaster.co.uk/news/2019/8/15/the-pugin-letters). Miss Coulston was the daughter of John Coulston, who had been the first Lancastrian philanthropist to offer money to provide a park for the people of Lancaster on the Moor (see John Coulston's munificent offer, p 35). Pugin also designed St Joseph's Church, built next door. He had occasion to write to the first Rector of the mission at St Joseph's about the length of time that it was taking to build the house, the cost of which was in the region of £2000, about £250,000 in today's money. He also wrote to Harrisons to warn that 'if the building is not completed in time the penalty will be enforced'.

William had moved into a large, relatively newly built house at 58 Regent Street by 1901. His occupation was listed as a master builder and the family had one domestic servant. Sadly, William died only two years later, at the age of 52.

The brother's two widows also had very different lives. Henry's widow, Jane, was working as a milliner at the age of 52 to support herself and still lived in a two-up two-down on De Vitre Street, while William's widow, Elizabeth, was listed as living on 'private means' in 1911, at 7 Lindow Square, a very respectable address just round the corner from her previous home on Regent Street.

Quarrying and the use of the resultant stone in building projects had resulted in William being able to provide very well for his widow. The tale of the Harrison family illustrates nicely how some in the Victorian era were able to thrive through hard work and also some luck, while others struggled through no fault of their own.

An injury to a young quarryman

Working the Moor quarries does seem to have been a dangerous occupation. In 1874, a 24-year-old man, Thomas Garth, of 6 Golgotha, 'was engaged in blasting some stone at the Moor Quarries, and was severely burnt about the face by the explosion which ensued. It had not fired as it ought to have done, and whilst he was removing the upper powder, it exploded and injured both his eyes'. He was taken to the Infirmary but, fortunately for him, it was not thought that the injuries would permanently affect his sight (*Lancaster Guardian* 10 January 1874). His mother, Nancy, was one of the laundresses of Golgotha village, next to what is now the Wyresdale Road entrance to the park.

Golgotha village in around 1927 (Lancaster City Museums LANLM.1945.8.269)

Golgotha was famous for being the home of many laundresses in the 1800s. In the 1881 census, Golgotha consisted of 22 cottages and out of the inhabitants of these, 16 women called themselves 'laundresses'. They used the surrounding fields as drying grounds. The cottages there were built between the late seventeenth century and the mid nineteenth century and may initially have been built to provide housing for quarry workers. Incidentally, in the same census, four stonemasons were listed as living there and two listed simply as 'stone quarries'.

DID YOU KNOW?

The place name Golgotha appears to relate to the position on the hill close to a place of execution, Gallows Hill (Golgotha being the name of the hill in Jerusalem on which Jesus was crucified), although the exact origin of the name isn't known for certain.

The cotton famine and its effects on the town of Lancaster

The mills of Lancaster and the Poor Law Act

The cotton famine became important in the history of the development of the park due to the provisions in the Poor Law Act which stipulated that manual labour must be given to out-of-work mill hands.

The interior of a cotton mill in the nineteenth century

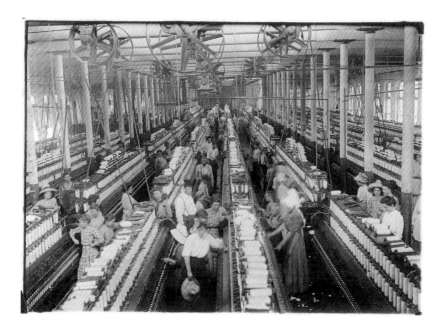

There were six mills involved in the cotton spinning industry in the nineteenth century, providing work to many of the people of Lancaster, and they were mainly situated along the canal. This work would have been extremely difficult and dangerous, involving thirteen-hour days in a literally deafening environment. The hot, humid and dust-filled air resulted in many illnesses, including lung diseases and cancer, while the moving machinery resulted in many terrible accidents, often fatal. This clip is from the *Lancaster Gazette* dated 29 November 1884, and the accident involved a small boy:

"Mill Accident – On Wednesday afternoon a lad ten years of age, named James Watson, whose parents reside in Primrose-street, met with a severe accident at Greenfield Mill, where he is employed. The lad was doing something about the machinery, when he was caught by a strap and drawn against a pulley, receiving severe injuries about the head and face. He was taken to the Infirmary, where he remains in a somewhat precarious condition."

The cotton famine lasted for a period of around four years in the early 1860s – it was a period of depression caused by the interruption of baled cotton imports from the USA during the American Civil War. The boom years of 1859 and 1860 had resulted in over-production of woven cotton, but the blockade of ports in the south of the USA caused the price of raw cotton to rise by several hundred per cent. This resulted in mill owners being unable to obtain supplies of raw cotton, leading to mill closures or short-term working.

Many mill workers were left destitute and in desperate circumstances.

In Lancaster the shortages of raw cotton had a major impact. In January 1862, the Reverend Alexander Page, vicar of St Anne's Chapel on Moor Lane, wrote to the *Lancaster Gazette* (25 January 1862) regarding the suffering of the out-of-work mill hands. He reported that at Bath Mill very few persons were working, many had been out of work for months and that at Queen Street Mill notice had been given that work would cease entirely in a short time.

He believed that the best way to give relief was by providing work for able-bodied men and proposed appeals for funds be raised to do this. He also suggested the opening of a soup kitchen so 'that wholesome food may be cheaply obtained', and for sewing classes to be formed for girls who were out of work. The clothes they made would be sold and the girls would receive 'some small pay' for their work. He finished by saying, 'Those who are in the habit of going amongst the poor will be able to testify that there is urgent need for some systemic relief being given to the increasing distress amongst us.'

DID YOU KNOW?

The Poor Law Board required those needing relief to be given some form of employment in order for relief to be provided. This was known as the 1842 Outdoor Labour Test Order and was put in place as there were not enough spaces in workhouses for all those needing relief during downturns in manufacturing. So able-bodied unemployed were offered relief in return for some form of deterrent manual labour, often stone-breaking or oakum picking, usually in a yard attached to the workhouse. At least half of the relief provided in this way had to be given in the form of food, clothing or other necessary articles.

He was not the only one concerned about providing aid to those in poverty as a result of the cotton famine in the town. In February of that year (*Lancaster Gazette* 8 February 1862) the Clerk to the Board of Guardians (a group of people elected in each parish to administer the Poor Law Act and to establish workhouses) was requested by the Mayor to report to a meeting of the Corporation. The Clerk reported that there were about 300 people out of employment in Lancaster, only 80 of them being men and the rest women and children. He explained that if the Board did not find work for them, the alternative was the workhouse. The unemployed made up only part of the total number of those in receipt of relief from the Guardians, however, as was reported in the *Lancaster Gazette* (shown in the excerpt below, 1 March 1862), which shows a slightly worse picture than for the previous year:

"State of Trade in Lancaster and the Pauperism –
The Silk Mills, Moor-lane Mills, and the White Cross
Mill are working full time. Mr. W. Jackson's hands
are employed four days per week, and the other two
mills – Queen's and Bath, which were standing, have
commenced working three days a week. The number
relieved by the Guardians was:-

	1862	1861
Jan.25	1039	1045
Feb.1	1073	998
Feb.8	1095	988
Feb.15	1091	989
Feb.22	1081	976

At the meeting with the Clerk to the Board of Guardians, it was clear that there was some suspicion among certain members of the Corporation that poor relief was 'much abused, the idle and the dissolute coming in for the best share'.

However, not all the members of the town's Corporation felt that way. It may be telling of his philanthropic attitude towards the town that at that same meeting, Mr James Williamson (the future donor of money to create the park), 'expressed his feeling that amongst many there was too great a spirit of independence to allow them to go to the Poor Law Guardians'. Overall, the feeling of the Corporation was that the full extent of the distress in the town did not come to the notice of the Board of Guardians, due to the reluctance of many in dire need to go to the relief office to ask for support. Then as now, many people were proud, and felt ashamed to be unable to provide for themselves.

The local Board of Health was also involved in providing paid work for those in need, but apparently not to the same extent as the Poor Law

Board. The figures given in the same newspaper article mentioned earlier
for February 1862 was sixteen, with fourteen outdoor and two indoor
able-bodied paupers being given work. However, this figure was to rise
substantially to 58 by the summer of that year.

Altogether, the Corporation felt that at this point in time things were
not that bad and that 'things had been much worse in the past'. They did
agree that those in need of relief should apply to the Board of Guardians
(i.e. the Poor Law Board) and they would be given paid work of some
kind, the 'Council being of the opinion that it was not their province to
take the initiative'. However, in 1863 the Corporation was sufficiently
concerned about the poor of the town to allow the building of a soup

Drunkenness at the Relieving Office

Richard Wilson was an unemployed factory operative who had had part-time work at
Queen Street Mill, but was also thought to have worked some days on the Moor. He
was charged with being drunk at the Relieving Office where he 'used very violent and
insulting language' and refused to leave. Mr Grant, Clerk to the Board of Guardians,
reported that Mr Wilson had earned nine shillings at the mill and could have earned
more if he had gone to work on the Moor. He further observed that 'during the present
depression there had been more riotous drunken conduct at the relieving office than
upon any former occasion.

'He did not apply it to the mill operatives out of work, for their conduct generally had
been very creditable, but in cases of this kind there were some who took advantage of
the benevolent, and gave way to vile offences.' (*Lancaster Gazette*, 24 May 1862)

kitchen on Common Garden Street, to be owned by the Corporation (*Committee Minute Books*, Lancashire Archives).

The park's first benefactor: John Coulston's 'Munificent Offer'

The idea of a park on Lancaster Moor was initially proposed as early as 1862. In April of that year Mr John Coulston wrote to the Mayor, Mr Henry Gregson, offering to contribute the sum of £500 (equivalent to around £60,000 today) towards converting some of the land on Lancaster Moor into 'pleasure grounds for the use of the public' (*Lancaster Guardian* 10 May 1862*).* He realised that this sum would not be sufficient on its own, saying in a letter in the newspaper that 'I have no doubt that your brother [Samuel Gregson, MP for Lancaster at the time], the member, and other wealthy individuals connected to Lancaster would be glad to subscribe to it liberally'. He went on: 'The grounds would afford the inhabitants *of all classes* an excellent place for exercise and recreation, and to strangers they would become an object of great attraction on account of the splendid views they would command.'

> DID YOU KNOW?
>
> John Coulston (1796–1866) was the manager of the Lancaster Banking Company on Church Street (now the NatWest bank) for forty years and was a member of a prominent nineteenth-century Catholic family who played an important part in the development of Catholic churches in the Lancaster area.

The Mayor responded to this letter by saying he himself had for a long time desired to convert the moor into pleasure and recreation grounds. At the Corporation meeting which followed, it was thought that they (the Corporation) ought to put down another £500 out of the rates to find employment for the poor and that they should 'make an arboretum of the Moor, plant it and make walks'. There was mention of earlier plans for various walks on the Moor; one from 1860 suggesting a walk on one side of the Moor, and another plan from 1861 which suggested a walk on the other side of the hill. However, it was agreed to start from scratch and maybe employ the services of a landscape gardener.

It was also mentioned that there should be no obstacle to obtaining the quarries as they were but little used (although the income from the quarries at this point was still around £40 per year and it was thought that the quarries could be carried on being worked during the construction of the park. *Lancaster Gazette* 7 June 1862). It was agreed to set up a special committee to oversee the formation of a park and it was hoped that their labours would result in a speedy 'setting of the shoulder to the wheel'. Unfortunately, for various reasons, as will be seen, this was not to be as simple a matter as was hoped.

Unemployed cotton mill workers are set to work

A month later, in June 1862, the Board of Health and the Board of Guardians agreed to liaise with each other in providing employment to able-bodied men who were out of work due to the depression in the cotton trade. The first task to be undertaken was that of 'removing the hill on the Moor-road near Highfield' (just to the west of Lancaster Cemetery) and it was agreed that the Board of Guardians would provide the relief due (i.e. pay the wages) under the Poor Law Act and that the Board of Health would supervise the work and provide the tools.

The Board of Health was particularly keen to know that outdoor relief would be provided for unmarried female mill hands and they were reassured that this would be the case. Whether this meant they were put to work on the roads is not clear. However, the *Lancaster Gazette* (2 July 1862) reported that the Board of Health was employing 58 men who had been thrown out of work by the depression in the cotton trade. It was stated that the greatest proportion of these were employed in the formation of a road from the entrance to the Cemetery to Golgotha, which skirted the wall to the Asylum grounds and which, when complete, 'will form a delightful promenade, the view from above the stone quarries being so extensive'. The present drive up to the Memorial from the Quernmore Road entrance still follows this route today, largely along the route of the old wall which divided the Moor land from the Asylum grounds. Other men were employed putting Vicarage Road and Marsh Lane in good order.

By August the Relief Fund Committee sent out a circular (now in Lancashire Archives) requesting subscriptions from those town-folk who were able to pay, in order that a fund could be set up to provide work for the unemployed mill operatives. The circular also stated 'There are 900 factory hands in Lancaster out of employment, and it is probable that, in a week or two, more.' The need for providing work for all these men was becoming more urgent.

The attitude of the Board of Guardians to the necessity of providing outdoor work for the indoor labourers was that it generally benefited them, but they stipulated that the work provided should not be beyond their capacity in kind or quantity, and that 'proper arrangements against undue exposure to inclement weather' should be made (*Lancaster Gazette* 23 August 1862).

> "It must be evident that to leave large numbers of men who are unaccustomed to anything but manual labour entirely unemployed, would not mitigate but rather aggravate and intensify the evils under which they suffer; and it has been found in many instances that such a state of things has produced great disorders.
>
> It is also clear that a life of inaction is calculated to lead to vicious pursuits, to debase and enervate the character, and to undermine industrious habits. The views of the Guardians in these respects are entertained by other experienced persons, and supported by positive evidence."

Lancaster Gazette clip 23 August 1862

It can be seen from the cutting shown above that it was felt that providing work would benefit the moral and social health of the unemployed, allowing them to 'retain their vigorous self-reliance and industrious habits' instead of their becoming demoralised and dependent paupers. Making sure that the able-bodied poor worked for their relief was felt to be very important to avoid engendering 'a spirit of deception, indolence, improvidence and pauperism'!

'Hard Times Walk'

By the winter of 1863/64 various other works had been carried out by the mill workers, including: the repair of the road from the river to Marsh Mill; repair of Vicarage Road, creating a new footpath in Freeman's Wood; the lowering of the hill at Highfield by around twelve feet; and last but not least, the creation of a footpath across the Moor which had become known, aptly, as 'Hard Times Walk'.

This was described in the *Lancaster Gazette* on 30 April 1864 as

> A walk which affords some of the finest prospects imaginable. From this cause, and the salubrity of the air to be inhaled in that elevated spot, and being within an easy distance of the town, this walk became exceedingly popular, and in fine weather was daily visited by hundreds either for pleasure or recreation.

The 'Albert Park' for Lancaster?

The Corporation considered naming Lancaster's proposed park 'Albert Park' in honour of Prince Albert, Queen Victoria's husband, who had died at the end of 1861 at the young age of 42 (*Lancaster Gazette* 12 July 1862). The other alternative under consideration as a proposed memorial to honour Albert's memory was a scholarship at the Grammar School. The Mayor felt that whichever scheme got the most subscriptions promised by the end of the council meeting should be the deciding factor, but said that calling the park the Albert Park would deprive Mr Coulston (who had offered £500 to the park scheme) of 'a right to which he was fairly entitled'. Maybe he felt that 'Coulston Park' was a possibility, but whatever the name, the Mayor considered that the park scheme would be best realised by raising a fund to aid those who were deprived of making a living as a result of the depression in the cotton trade. It was also argued that this would not exclude the park being named the Albert Park in memorial to Prince Albert.

Some observed that the Moor was already a place 'in which inhabitants of all classes might enjoy the fresh air' and that as a recreation ground in its state at the time (the Moor did have a 'walk' upon it, but the quarries were still being worked) was already 'an outlet for the inhabitants of the town who were confined in the courts and alleys'. It was even suggested that the folk of Lancaster could go to the cemetery if they wanted fresh air! It must be remembered that the town at that time would have been a dirty and smoky environment.

Eventually the Committee came to a vote and it was split fifteen votes to fifteen for each scheme. The Mayor, Mr Henry Gregson, had the casting vote and he voted in favour of the Grammar School Scholarship (£266 being subscribed to this immediately after the meeting) and so the 'Albert Park' never came to be.

Thomas Storey's support for the park

Thomas Storey was one of the founders of Storey Brothers in Lancaster, manufacturers of table baize and oil cloth, which grew to become one of Lancaster's largest employers by the end of the century, the firm carrying on in business until 1977.

In August 1862 Thomas Storey was in correspondence with Lancaster's MP, William Garnett (letters held at Lancashire Archives), in support of 'the conversion of part of the moor into ornamental pleasure recreation grounds' and 'thereby to provide labour for the unemployed operatives'. He promised to donate £100 to the scheme, in addition to Mr Coulston's £500, stating that he felt that 'this is a time when one will have to make sacrifices one way or another'. He wrote to Mr Garnett again in September, stating that a portion of the Moor could be well-adapted for a cricket ground and saying that he was keen to discuss this with the MP when he next saw him. His wishes for this particular use of the Moor never materialised.

Edward Kemp: the park's first landscape architect

As early as June 1862 it was agreed by the Corporation that the first objective in planning the new park would be to 'employ an experienced practical man to give a plan and an approximate estimate'. By October it was reported that a sub-committee had been formed to confer with Mr Coulston over the park plans but that nothing had yet been done! However, they had 'had a gentleman over to inspect the Moor, and all the remark he made was that they must be careful not to destroy nature: nature had done so much they must be careful not to destroy it' (*Lancaster Gazette* 11 December 1862). Whether or not this was the landscape gardener who eventually produced the plan is not clear. However, not much progress was made until the following year.

By August 1863 it was reported that a Mr Kemp, landscape gardener, had been commissioned to prepare plans for the Moor. When he visited to inspect the area, Alderman Gregson had gone to the Moor with Mr Kemp (*Lancaster Gazette* 31 October 1863) and it was found that in laying it out for a park it would not require any extensive planting. After several letters to chase them up, his plans were recorded as having been received by the Corporation.

Mr Kemp was a prominent landscape gardener at the time he was commissioned to make plans for Lancaster Moor, and was one of the leading park designers of parks and gardens during the mid-Victorian era in England. He had written a book entitled *How to Lay Out a Garden* in 1858, and in 1855 he had designed the grounds at Capernwray Hall near Carnforth for the Marton family. In 1843, at the age of 25, he was employed to implement the plans of Joseph Paxton (another prominent landscape gardener) for the laying out of Birkenhead Park in Liverpool, where he was subsequently retained as Park Superintendent.

Unfortunately, his plans for Lancaster Moor cannot be traced, but an illustration from his book shows a layout for an estate named Shendish in Hertfordshire 'where the house [has been] erected on the summit of a hill, where there was an excellent platform for the purpose, and from whence the ground descends'. This layout included curving driveways and one can imagine from this a similar design for the Moor land.

For some reason it was another four years before the Improvement Committee of the Corporation agreed to forward Mr Kemp's bill for the park plans to the Finance Committee for payment. The bill amounted to £25 10s. 9d. (*Committee Minutes Book* 13 November 1866).

An old stone bench with a mysterious inscription

Situated near the top of the drive from the back of the Memorial leading down towards the lake there is a mysterious stone bench bearing the cryptic inscription 'Rev. T. R. London 1863'. One might assume that this is a memorial to a Reverend London who died in 1863, but this is not the case.

Stone bench with inscription Rev. T. R. London

The truth is that it was donated to the park by the Reverend Thomas Richardson (*Lancaster Gazette* 7 February 1863) who was born in Lancaster in 1830 (as shown in the 1881 census). His father was a cabinet maker and they lived on Friar Street. Thomas became a vicar in the East End of London at various churches, including St George in the East (See stgitehistory.org.uk/stmatthewpellstreet.html) and St Benet's in Stepney. He was known to have preached at the Garrick and other theatres, and afterwards attendance at his church grew, 'the increase [being] from the lowest orders'.

He learnt German in order to hold wedding services for the local German population, who attended his church due

Portrait of Rev. T. Richardson

Stone bench outside the park gates on Wyresdale Road

Stone bench covered in vegetation

to the fees at the German Church being so high! He also established a branch of the Band of Hope (a temperance organisation for working class children) and once walked from Bournemouth to London handing out religious tracts.

Interestingly there are two other stone benches of similar design but without an inscription, one just outside the park gates at Golgotha, and another (almost engulfed by vegetation) on the left-hand side of the main drive from the Quernmore Road entrance, which seem to date from the same period.

These three stone benches are among the earliest features of the park and are marked on the 1877 Harrison and Hall map of Lancaster as small rectangles (see p 64).

There is a fourth identical stone bench situated near the Lancaster Royal Grammar School, at the junction of Quernmore Road and Wyresdale Road.

Delays in developing the moor into a park

Trouble with commonable rights

Commons are areas where certain people hold beneficial rights to use land that they do not own, and this was the case with much of the land on Lancaster Moor. In Lancaster, freemen of the borough and landowners in the townships of Lancaster, Skerton and Slyne-with-Hest all held commonable rights to graze cattle on the land of Lancaster Moor.

The first mention of potential problems arising due to claims for commonable rights on the Moor was in June of 1862, when the townships of Slyne-with-Hest and Skerton both established their claims over rights on the Moor land. By the following year this matter was still not settled. If the claims to the land were not transferred to the Corporation willingly, compulsory powers could only be got by an Act of Parliament, which would take time, and it seems that not much discussion had yet occurred with the various groups who had claims (*Lancaster Gazette* 15 August 1863). Matters were not resolved with regard to this until years later.

Financing the park

Although Mr Coulston had promised the sum of £500, this alone was not going to be sufficient for the Corporation's scheme. However, there was inevitable disagreement within the Corporation about how to raise further sums (*Lancaster Guardian* 15 August 1863). One option

was to borrow money from the
Government under the Public
Works Act, which would have
meant work could start sooner.
The other option was to raise
funds by subscriptions from
benefactors, or by raising a local
tax. It was thought that at least
£1000 would be needed to form a
simple recreation ground, more for
a people's park.

By October 1863 Mr Coulston
had understandably become fed
up of waiting for the Corporation
to make progress with the Moor plans – it was by then eighteen months
since he had pledged £500 to the project, an offer he then withdrew.
The reasons he gave were the difficult question over the ownership of the
land and his doubts over the ability of the Council to enclose the land
(i.e. settle the commonable rights over the land).

Initial steps in the creation of the park

So now the Corporation had the plans for their park but no funds! For this reason, the Corporation decided not to use Mr Kemp's plans in their entirety, but to use portions of them that winter, as the Relief Committee had requested some work for the unemployed. The funds from the Relief Committee were now the only funds available for the work. They would be able to commence within two weeks, and it was suggested they began with the 'large carriage road marked upon the plan as commencing near the reservoir' as this would not affect the workings of the quarries.

A public meeting was held and 'so great was the sympathy displayed on behalf of the suffering operatives, that in a short time a very handsome sum was raised … Lancaster resolutely determined *not to accept any relief from the central fund, but to maintain its own poor by its own subscriptions*' (*Lancaster Gazette* 30 April 1864).

The state of the Moor at this point in time was described vividly by Thomas Storey: 'At present any one that took them could pick here and pick there, until the place presented the appearance of a lot of pigs rooting up the ground' (*Lancaster Gazette* 31 October 1863).

This was probably in part due to the fact that the quarries were being let for short terms only, usually as little as one month (*Lancaster Gazette* 19 March 1864), and this caused the stonemasons of the town some problems. More importantly for the development of the park, it was thought that the quarries could continue to be worked without interfering with the proposed improvements.

'Shakespeare Road' – a carriage drive is constructed

With what seems like great pomp and ceremony, the progress of the new carriage drive on the Moor was inspected on 28 April 1864, the formal opening not being due to be held until Whit Monday (16 May). The road commenced at what is now the entrance gate to the park on Quernmore Road and proceeded in a winding direction to join up with the footpath already created and known as 'Hard Times Walk', about halfway up the hill. The two then joined and carried on up to the summit as a metalled carriageway of 18 feet in width.

This 'inspection' was carried out by the Mayor, members of the Relief Committee and other dignitaries of the town. They met at the Poor Law Office in town and were then taken by 'five carriages and pairs' generously provided by Mr Sly, proprietor of the King's Arms Hotel (*Lancaster Gazette* 30 April 1864). When this procession of five carriages arrived at the summit of the hill, 'they alighted on the green and from one of the carriages was brought a few bottles of wine for the friends and a supply of bread and cheese and ale for the workmen'. Toasts were drunk to the health of the Queen and the Mayor and a vote of thanks was given to the Relief Committee. Various other toasts followed, after which the company returned to town in their carriages and were hospitably entertained by Mr Sly at the King's Arms.

The *Lancaster Gazette* reported that they had been asked 'to convey the thanks of the poor men, the workers on the moor, to those gentlemen by whom their unexpected feast of bread and cheese and ale was provided. That kindness will long be remembered by them.' The vote of thanks seems a little excessive, given that the well-to-do were being fed and watered free of charge at the King's Arms!

Further plans for the park at that time, according to the *Gazette*, were to carry on the carriage road towards Golgotha by way of a gentle descent and also 'to level a large space on the summit of the hill [the eventual site of the Ashton Memorial] for a promenade, and to provide for the amusement of youth by the formation of quoiting grounds' and spaces for 'nine holes in some of the many dells which abound there'. They also suggest that no more

> ### DID YOU KNOW?
>
> It seems that the Shakespeare Road must have been so named because 1864 was the tercentenary of William Shakespeare's birth.

'whins' (gorse bushes) should be burned in order to preserve the beauty of the moor, 'adding as they do a picturesque appearance to the charms of the surrounding scenery'.

Unfortunately, the grand opening of the Shakespeare Road originally proposed by the Mayor for Whit Monday did not take place. It was delayed in order to wait for its completion across the Moor to Golgotha. It is not clear exactly when this opening did take place, but it was probably at least not until the following year, as the Improvement Committee of the Corporation requested that 'the Surveyor inspect the course of the roads now being made by the Guardians on the Moor' in May 1865 (*Committee Minute Books*, Lancashire Archives).

Throughout the rest of the 1860s, problems with enclosing the land on the Moor in order to make a park rumbled on, together with debate over the use of Mr Coulston's gift of £500. Mr Coulston had died in 1866, but his sister, Miss Anne Coulston, was keen that this sum of money be put to good use (*Lancaster Gazette* 17 October 1868). There had previously been disagreement between Mr Coulston and the Corporation – he had threatened to take action against them over ownership of the land after the Board of Health had organised the making of the footpath on some of the Moor land. An agreement was eventually reached with him over his right to the land (the Corporation paid him £20 an acre on the understanding that he was promising the £500 towards the development of a park). The *Lancaster Gazette* reported in 1870 that Miss Coulston was still willing for the Corporation to have the £500 as long as they could meet her brother's original request that 'subscriptions be obtained equivalent to the amount of the estimated cost of the intended gardens, on a plan to be furnished by Mr Kemp, including trees, planting, and every other item of expense'. Miss Coulston had said her brother had mentioned to her that £2000 was the minimum amount that ought to be available and she therefore stipulated that a sum of £1500 ought to be raised within two years or her offer would be withdrawn (*Lancaster Gazette* 15 October 1870). It seems that the Corporation never did manage to raise the funds.

Dangerous quarries on 'Hard Times Walk' and further delays

In February 1868 the dangers of the open quarries were apparent – the *Lancaster Gazette* described a deep unused quarry as being totally unprotected and only feet away from the road (*Lancaster Gazette* 15 February 1868). Railings to protect the public had not been put up as it was thought they would be an inducement to children to climb on them, but it was fortunate that no-one had been injured or worse in a fall.

The quarries were also collecting water, making them difficult to work, and the Mayor complained that tenants had 'been digging about wherever they liked'. It was agreed that a plan be prepared for the future working of the quarries. It was obviously intended that the quarries would continue to be worked for a good few years, as in 1868 agreements were signed to let the North Quarry for four years and the South Quarry for five years (*Lancaster Gazette* 11 July 1868).

By 1870 the rights over the use of the land on the Moor were still not agreed and some in the Corporation did not appear to be in any hurry to resolve matters. The Town Clerk was in communication with interested parties but was reported as saying 'It had gone on very satisfactorily, but they could not possibly come to a conclusion all at once. If they allowed it to go on, no doubt in the end they should be enabled to effect a very satisfactory arrangement' (*Lancaster Gazette* 13 August 1870). Not surprisingly, it would be another five years before the Corporation found a solution to the problem of enclosing the land on the Moor.

It appears that some local farmers who claimed to have commonable rights over the Moor in fact didn't. The Council put pressure on some local farmers to withdraw their claims to have rights to use the land, an example of this being reported in the Committee Minute Books for 1870. A Mr Martin Ireland, a farmer at Nightingale Hall Farm, had to agree to drop his claim to rights over the land on the Moor under threat of action against him for trespass for putting sheep there. The Committee resolved 'That Ireland be required to sign an Admission in Writing of the Trespass, of his withdrawal of any Claim to Rights of Common and also to pay a sum to cover the costs of Writ and other Expenses.' (*Committee Minutes Book*, Lancashire Archives).

The Army requests some of the Moor land for a barracks

In 1873 some of the Moor adjacent to the Asylum was almost sold to the Army, who wanted about 10 acres of land to build a barracks. At this point the Asylum buildings were yet to be extended and only existed on the same side of Quernmore Road as the park.

The Corporation did not agree to sell them this land as 'it was wanted for other purposes' (*Lancaster Gazette* 11 January 1873), presumably to create the park.

Others in the town disagreed and thought that they should sell the land, believing that they may as well make some money out of it, as they considered the land was not suitable for a park (*Lancaster Gazette* 25 January 1873). Some of the reasons given for this opinion were the exposed position, the steep 'toilsome' approach from the town, and the expense that would be involved in creating a park. As one writer correctly pointed out, for a generation all that had happened was talk! Another writer to the *Gazette* stated that the objections raised to the sale of the land – that it was used by youths from the town for recreation– was false and that he had only seen patients from the Asylum playing cricket there. Eventually a compromise was reached and land to the west of Golgotha was used for the barracks. These still exist and are now part of the University of Cumbria.

DID YOU KNOW?

The Asylum, or Lancaster County Lunatic Asylum as it was first known (in more recent times known as Lancaster Moor Hospital), was built in 1816 on a site just to the north-east of the Moor quarry lands. This oldest part of the Moor Hospital closed in 1991 and is now a housing estate, Standen Park, some parts of the Georgian buildings having been retained. The huge extension to the Asylum on the other side of Quernmore Road, was completed in 1883 and was known as the 'Annexe'. This part of Lancaster Moor hospital had closed by 2000 and has now been converted into apartments, known as The Residence. At its peak in the 1940s, the Asylum housed up to 3,400 patients in its various buildings and was one of the largest such institutions in the country. The surrounding land has now become part of the park; see the section on Fenham Carr.

"A HAWK SHOT ON THE MOOR – A few days ago a fine specimen of the kestrel hawk, which had been noticed by severak persons hovering about the quarries on the moor, was shot by Mr. R. R. Hathornthwaite, of Highfield. The bird was twice shot at without any effect at a long range, and then, as if in illustration of the proverb – "familiarity breeds contempt," ventured within about thirty yards of the gun, when a third shot brought him down with a good fifty feet fall into the bottom of an old quarry. It is not often that a hawk is to be seen in the vicinity of "Hard Times," and still rarer that a bird of the kind should be shot at three times in one day and eventually killed. The specimen has been very successfully stuffed by Mr Sanderson, of Chapel-street, and will form an interesting memento of a morning's sport among the quarries."

Above is a *Lancaster Gazette* report from 11 December 1875 about a rare sighting of a hawk in the vicinity of 'Hard Times Walk'. It was shot at three times and eventually killed by a Mr Hathornthwaite, later to be stuffed by a Mr Sanderson of Chapel Street.

The state of the Moor in 1875, and one man's ambitious plans

A very descriptive letter was written to the *Lancaster Gazette* (14 August 1875) urging the town of Lancaster to facilitate the creation of the park on the Moor. It was signed 'A Freeman of Lancaster' and it is nice to think that this freeman may have been James Williamson himself, whom we shall see eventually did indeed facilitate the creation of the park two years later.

The letter first gave a vivid description of the land as it then stood, as consisting merely of various 'footways appropriately described as 'Hard Times' and a couple of seats, one of stone (presumably that donated by Rev. Richardson) and one of iron. His letter continued to describe the impression that the condition of the Moor would give to visitors to the town:

> How strange that the town should appear so neglectful of the splendid site. What irregular mounds and unsightly heaps of broken stone. Quarrymen have for generations past been engaged in breaking up the layers of stone and piling up the fragments *anyhow* ... mounds half-coated with whin bushes ... It might seem as if a set of gigantic children had been playing at 'making hills'. Here and there may be seen a rude hut of wood, a large crane, and the splintered effects of a recent blast. On the side of Golgotha, a solitary ass, a few green geese, and one or two hen-houses of wood, complete the peculiar mixture of the whole prospect, in contrast to the well-ordered grounds of the Asylum. If one thing strikes the tourist, it is that Lancaster is dead to her own interests on the side of the Moor, and also to the comfort of her numerous visitors.

Secondly, the mysterious letter-writer went on to describe his ambitious vision for the park. Some quotes from his letter are as follows:

> We ought, on immediately ascending beyond the Workhouse, to come within view of one of the finest Parks in the county, elegantly diversified with beautiful lawns, gravelled walks, artificial sheets of water and grottoes. The existing unevenness of the ground can be taken advantage of as far as possible ... Stony retreats will form most admirable caves, where collections of various curiosities can be stored ... A few arbours encircled with jasmine and honeysuckle, a Swiss cottage or two, and a Chinese tower of the Kew fashion.

He went further and became ever more ambitious in his desires for the park:

DID YOU KNOW?

The workhouse was situated on a site now occupied by Lancaster Royal Grammar School, just above the junction of Wyresdale Road and Quernmore Road and opposite Christ Church.

a few swans and foreign ducks, an aviary well-stocked with
parrots, even a menagerie, with an extensive monkey-house
– at least a few climbing bears in deep well-like dens …
There is no reason why a public gymnasium should not be
added or a good bowling-green.

He finished by saying, 'I appeal to all spirited and patriotic men in
Lancaster and in the Corporation to join in the furtherance of this great
and advantageous scheme.'

The Lancaster Water and Improvement Act

In 1875 Lancaster Corporation finally got organised and applied to
Parliament for a Bill to empower the Corporation to compulsorily
purchase the land on Lancaster Moor and to revoke 'all commonable or
other rights' (*Lancaster Gazette* 13 November 1875). The proposed Bill
also included a section allowing them to convert this land to a pleasure or
recreation ground:

> To empower the Corporation to appropriate and maintain as
> public walks, pleasure, or recreation ground, all or any part
> of Lancaster Moor, and to lay out, fence, drain, level, plant,
> and improve the same, and to make rides, drives, walks, and
> ponds, and all appropriate buildings and conveniences …

There was also a clause to allow the Corporation to sell any portions of
the Moor not required for public walks, pleasure or recreation grounds
as they may think fit. This bill was known as the 'Lancaster Water and
Improvement Act' and also provided for such things as the construction
of new water conduits and aqueducts, to charge rates for the supply of
water and to make and maintain various street improvements.

So, there was now an Act in place to enclose the land on the Moor, but
no money with which to carry out the plans.

A smallpox hospital is built on the Moor

In October 1877 (*Lancaster Gazette* 17 October 1877), a very strongly worded anonymous letter from 'Sunshine' was published in the *Lancaster Gazette* criticising the Corporation for building a 'A Monument of Folly' upon the Moor. It described the Corporation as showing a high capacity for blundering. It seems that plans had been made to build a permanent infectious diseases hospital elsewhere, but the plans were quietly dropped in the hope that the hospital would not become necessary. Then, when a smallpox epidemic took hold, the Council hastily erected a temporary wooden structure on the Moor in a position which had 'justly been regarded as the people's recreation ground'.

He stated: 'What can visitors from a distance think of our intelligence when we put up a smallpox hospital in such a situation' and called for the removal of this 'objectionable eyesore'.

> "THE SMALL-POX HOSPITAL – The Lancaster Town Council have determined to proceed with the erection of a small-pox hospital on the Moor! If there should be necessity for its use, this favourite recreation ground will have to be avoided as a focus of infection. What about a Moor Park? A small-pox hospital in the centre would neither be ornamental nor desirable. Verily, the dreams of the last few years are being rudely dispelled."

A *Lancaster Gazette* article from 14 July 1877

The hospital was eventually built on a site on the Marsh estate in 1880.

Theft of hens from the Moor

In 1877 the land on Lancaster Moor was not only still being quarried, but livestock was being kept there by some of the quarrymen. The *Lancaster Gazette* (24 February 1877) reported the theft of three hens belonging to John Makerell, a quarryman of Park Road, who was a foreman at the quarry of Messrs Briggs and Lancaster on Lancaster Moor. He stated that he 'had eleven hens and two cocks' locked up in the smithy at the quarry. The next day three hens were missing and William Miller, a labourer of Sugar House Alley, was discovered by his landlady to have a hen in a slop bucket; she told him to take it away. A police sergeant named Winder went in search of the missing hens, finding them in a cellar of an empty house close to where Miller lodged. The unfortunate Mr Miller was found guilty and given a harsh sentence of three months' hard labour at the castle.

The park's second benefactor: James Williamson

James Williamson and his offer of £10,000

Alderman James Williamson was born in 1813, the son of a woollen merchant from Keswick. The family came to Lancaster in the late 1820s, where James was apprenticed to a master painter and decorator. He then spent some time in London, where he observed the production of oilcloth and, upon his return to Lancaster, he perfected a process for producing this cheaply (*St George's Works Mill*, LDHG). He began

producing it in the late 1840s and was so successful that in 1854 he expanded his business by building St George's Mill on the Quay (sadly demolished in 2018), also producing table baize. The family lived at 1 Cable Street in Lancaster, and by 1871 the census returns list him as a Borough Magistrate, Alderman and manufacturer employing upwards of 800 hands. Clearly by then a wealthy and prominent member of Lancaster society.

James Williamson Snr (Lancaster City
Museums LANLM.1931.14.9)

By 1875 his son, James Williamson Jnr (later to become Lord Ashton), had taken control of the business due to his father's ill health and James Snr eventually died in 1879.

In October 1877 there were exciting developments in the history of Lancaster Moor.

James Williamson Snr was about to travel to Europe for the winter, but before leaving he handed a sealed document to the Mayor, asking him to open it at the next Council meeting, which he did (*Lancaster Gazette* 20 October 1877). The document was a letter, addressed to the Mayor, asking the Council to sell Alderman Williamson a portion of land on Lancaster Moor of around 40 acres, the land to be free from commonable rights. If they agreed to this request, he promised to spend a sum of not less than £10,000 (equivalent to over £1 million today (officialdata.org)) on converting the land into a 'public park or pleasure ground'. He also pledged to provide a maintenance fund and to hand the park back to the Corporation on its completion, suggesting that this could take around three years.

He closed the letter by offering another £500 towards providing a new covered market for the town as an 'inducement'.

The members of the Corporation present at that meeting were understandably both surprised and overwhelmed by James Williamson's offer, one of the councillors stating that he hoped the provision of a public park would encourage 'young men of social habits' out of public houses where they now obtained their 'social intercourse'. He went on to say, 'he hoped and believed that it would be a very effectual means of lessening that attendance in public houses which often led to such immoral and deplorable results'. This statement was met with applause.

It was mentioned that it was now some twenty years since a previous attempt to convert the Moor, which was 'abortive for many reasons', and that the idea of a park 'was again revived half-a-dozen years ago'. The Lancaster Water and Improvement Act put in place the previous year now enabled the Corporation to obtain the land and revoke commonable rights. Although similar words had been said before, on this occasion the words soon became actions, and a special committee was then formed to deal with the sale of the land. Mr Roper (one of the councillors on that special committee) then described the Moor as: 'A lung, an extra lung to the town of Lancaster' and stated that 'such a park would be a great benefit to the present and all future generations'.

The elder Williamson's poor health at that time (he was then aged 64) seems to have been the reason for his trip abroad for the winter, as Mr Roper hoped that he would return in the spring in 'health and strength'.

The enclosure of the land on the Moor

About three months later, the Corporation arranged separate meetings with the four groups of local people who were entitled to claim commonable rights on Lancaster Moor – freemen of the borough, and landholders in the townships of Lancaster, Skerton, and Slyne-with-Hest. The outcome was the formation of three separate committees; one for the freemen, and one each for Skerton and Lancaster landowners (no-one had attended the meeting for Slyne-with-Hest). These committees would negotiate with the Corporation over compensation (*Lancaster Gazette* 23 January 1878).

The Skerton landowners soon found a problem with their promised compensation and a meeting was called to be held in the schoolroom at Skerton to discuss reports that the agreed sum of £350 was to be spent outside the township. The Skerton landowners present felt that the money 'should be for Skerton and no other place' and should be spent in improving Skerton's schools (*Lancaster Gazette* 15 June 1878). One of the school governors, a Mr Hall, said in relation to this, 'If any of them went into the room adjoining that in which they then were when the infants were assembled, they would be horrified almost at the number of small children packed in there.' It was agreed unanimously that the compensation money should be applied to the improvement and enlargement of the school rooms.

Just over a year later the *Lancaster Gazette* (25 October 1879) reported the formal re-opening of the enlarged St Luke's School in Skerton, an event that was celebrated with a tea party for 400 people held in the school. The money to carry out the works had to be raised by voluntary contributions and these efforts resulted in the sum of £569. The article reported that Reverend John Brack, vicar of St Luke's, gave a speech and mentioned the failure to pay compensation money due to Skerton: '£350 would have been very nice if we could have got it, but we have not got it yet, and I don't know whether we ever shall. I can say, however, Mr Williamson (James Williamson Jnr) said 'If you don't get it, I will make up what you want to the tune of £200.' It is not known if the compensation money was ever received by the townspeople of Skerton.

Controversy over turning the Moor into a park

Two opposing views on the Moor as a park were made clear in the local newspapers' correspondence pages. On 29 June 1878 the *Lancaster Guardian* published a letter entitled 'What is a White Elephant?' from someone who called themselves 'An Old Lancastrian'. He considered that the Moor was already open to inhabitants of Lancaster to admire the scenery, and that the loss of the quarries would affect the poorest most, due to the increased cost of building materials for housing feeding through into higher rents: 'It is now a difficult thing to meet with a cottage under 5s a week fit for a family – the impending 10% reduction in the wages of the cotton operatives will not make it easier.'

In response to this letter, a week later the *Gazette* (6 July 1878) published a strongly-worded letter from a citizen signing themselves as 'A Few Facts', stating that it was clear to him who wrote the initial letter. He called the writer's attempts at wit 'stale and unprofitable' and mentioned a sum of £300 which 'An Old Lancastrian' described as a scholarship promised to the Grammar School. The writer of the second letter understood that this sum was actually part of the compensation money due to Skerton township and that the Skerton landowners were taking proceedings to ensure that it was used for their sole benefit.

He went on to dispute the high value that 'An Old Lancastrian' put on the stone left in the quarries and stated that, in fact, the stonemasons reported that the quarries were worn out.

He felt that the £1,000 offered by James Williamson to compensate for the loss of the quarries was generous and that there were other sources of stone in the town, including land adjoining the Scotch quarries which had 'an immense bed of stone'. He finished by saying that he was not clear why the editor of the *Guardian* (who he mentioned was a member of the Parks Committee) published the letter and that 'its insertion would give pain to the donor [of the money to create the park] who is now stricken down by sickness'.

> ### DID YOU KNOW?
>
> Scotch quarry was on land to the east of Primrose and Moorland estates and is now Scotch Quarry Urban Park and does lie 'below Golgotha'.

Boundary lines for park agreed

That same month, and nine months after the Corporation accepted Mr Williamson's gift, there was now a plan showing the outline of the area to be sold to Mr Williamson for the park (see image) which included all the Moor quarries (*Lancaster Gazette* 20 July 1878), the land being wedged in-between the County Asylum to the east and the Workhouse to the west.

Mr Williamson was present at this meeting and had wanted more land to be added to the proposed park area, such as 'the quarry below

Image from Deeds for area of land to be sold to James Williamson for the park (Reproduced with permission from Lancashire Archives, Lancashire County Council ref DDX909 acc11506/box3)

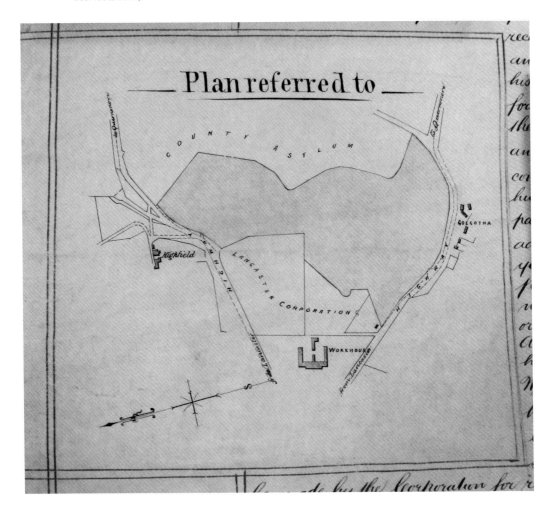

Golgotha', but it was agreed that this was not feasible. Some members of the Committee and the Surveyor had been up to the Moor and a road 48 feet in width had been marked out, running from the service reservoir just above the Workhouse (now part of the Grammar School) to the bottom of the hill beyond Golgotha – now known as Wyresdale Road.

By November, a draft deed had been prepared and agreed with Mr Williamson, apart from one point – the name of the park. The Town Clerk had sent the draft deed to Mr Williamson with a blank space for him to fill in the name, but he had returned it still blank. Councillor Abraham Seward suggested that the 'natural title will be the Williamson Park' and this suggestion was met with cries of 'Hear, hear' and applause (*Lancaster Gazette* 23 November 1878).

The deed was to the effect that the Corporation would hand over to Mr Williamson for three years, possession and exclusive control of the land and that he in his turn would expend at least £10,000 in improving it, and to establish a sufficient maintenance fund so as to relieve the Corporation of that burden.

James Williamson Jnr takes over

Unfortunately, James Williamson Senior died on 3 January 1879 (*Lancaster Gazette* 8 January 1879) but his son, also James (later Lord Ashton), stepped in to fulfil his father's wishes on the completion of the park. James Williamson Jnr also increased the sum set aside from his father's estate for the formation of the park by another £5,000, as it was realised that the initial £10,000 promised by his father would not be sufficient. He later proved to be as generous as his father by also increasing the amount donated for the subsequent maintenance of the park.

The map prepared by the Lancaster land agents' firm of Harrison and Hall in 1877 shows that the quarries were still present at that time. It also demonstrates the course of the carriage drive made across the top of the Moor in 1864, following the line of the wall separating the quarry area from the Asylum grounds at the bottom of the plan. The stone benches mentioned earlier are seen as tiny black rectangles on the map overleaf. The second bench from the top has been removed at some point.

Inspection of designs for the lodges, gateways and boundary walls

By April 1879, plans for the new park had moved on apace, and the Town Council met at Greenfield Mill on Moor Lane to inspect those for the entrance gateways, lodges and boundary walls (*Lancaster Gazette* 12 April 1879). They had been drawn up by Mr Huntington, joiner and builder, of Penny Street. The plans were for two entrances to the park, one on the Golgotha side and one on the Cemetery side, each with a lodge, to be

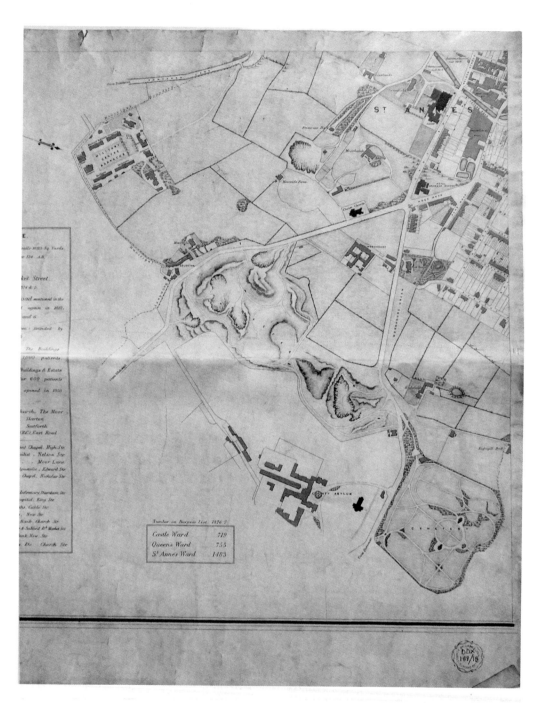

1877 Harrison and Hall map showing the quarries on Lancaster Moor (the tiny black rectangles indicate the position of the old stone benches) (Reproduced with permission from Lancashire Archives, Lancashire County Council, ref DDX/189/18)

exact copies of each other, the only difference being that the lodge at the Golgotha entrance was to be on the right side, while that for the lodge at the Cemetery entrance would be on the left.

The entrances consist of a stone archway under which are two sets of ornamental iron gates, the main one for carriages and the side ones for pedestrians. On a plain stone panel over the archway on the left is cut the word 'Williamson' and on the right 'Park 1880'. The upper portions of the carriageway gates carry shields, one of which is the arms of Alderman James Williamson and the other those of the Borough of Lancaster. The iron work was made at the Helix Furnace Feeder Company's works at Bath Mill. The gateways as originally planned are still *in situ*.

The substantial lodge buildings were to be identical – downstairs a living room, a bedroom, a kitchen and larder, and also 'the usual outdoor appurtenances of a modern dwelling house' – presumably an outdoor loo! Upstairs there were to be two more bedrooms. Note there is no bathroom, not unusual for those days.

The shields on the entrance gateways to the park, on the left the arms of James Williamson and on the right the arms of Lancaster Borough

The *Gazette* also reported that the conversion of the Moor into a park was being carried out under the superintendence of Mr McLean, landscape gardener of Derby, and that considerable progress had already been made with the formation of the carriage drive.

Mr MacLean: landscape gardener

In the 1871 census returns Mr John M(a)cLean is described as a market gardener, born in Scotland, and living on Park Road in Castle Donington in Leicestershire. But by 1881, the year after the park gates were installed, he is listed as a visitor at the newly completed Williamson Park Lodge, Golgotha, and his occupation is now given as landscape gardener. The resident of the Lodge is recorded as Peter Whieldon, a public park gardener, and his wife Fanny, who is listed as born in Castle Donington. In the same year, Mr McLean's wife and family are shown as having moved to Donington Park itself. In the *Kelly's Directory* for 1876 and 1881, John McLean is listed as a gardener at Donington Park. This connection with Castle Donington suggests that the staff for laying out the park were 'borrowed' from Donington Park, presumably due to some connection between James Williamson Jnr and Lord Donington ('Who was Mr McLean of Castle Donington?' Andrew White, *Contrebis* vol 26, 2001).

At the other Park Lodge in 1881 lived John Smart, landscape gardener, and his family. The work done by these gardeners in laying out the park is praised in the *Lancaster Guardian* (3 December 1881):

> As far as design was concerned the Park was left to design itself, Mr Maclean, under whose direction the Park was laid out, following as far as possible, and with beneficial effect, the conformation of the ground as he found it. Altogether the Park is a place of great beauty … It may be added that Mr Smart rendered great assistance to Mr Maclean in the work of laying out and constructing the Park.

May 1880: the park is half-completed

The *Lancaster Guardian* reported on 8 May 1880 that around half of the park was completed, the work requiring a huge amount of labour due to both the size of the park and the rugged nature of the ground:

> Several of the great hollows or valleys have been smoothed
> down, trimmed and ornamented, and great blocks of
> unhewn rock stand here and there as buttresses to the sides
> of chasms or break the monotony of long heathery slopes.

> Many thousands of shrubs and saplings have already been
> planted in the places available for shrubbery or coppice.

On the same date, the *Guardian* reported that the residents of Golgotha,
well known for its many washerwomen, at first objected to the park
because they used part of the Moor land as their drying ground. However,
they rented a large field on land belonging to the Coulston trustees and
laid it out 'in long lines or streets of stout poles, and the lines fastened to
them are of strong wire'. This action resolved their objection.

Transfer of the park to the town in 1881

The transfer of the land back to the town finally took place the following
year on 21 November 1881 (*Lancaster Gazette* 26 November 1881),
without ceremony at a meeting in the Town Hall. Mr Williamson had
requested that there should be no public celebration and had wished the
transfer to coincide with the exact date of the agreement between his
father and the Corporation three years earlier (Mr Williamson Snr had
previously stated that the park should be completed within three years).

James Williamson Jnr was not present at the meeting, but had
written a letter to the Mayor formally handing the completed park back
to the Corporation on behalf of the town. He enclosed a statement of
expenditure (see overleaf), which left a balance of £1,769 out of the sum
of £15,000. He stated that he felt this was not a sufficient amount for a
maintenance fund and promised to make this sum up to £10,000.

"SUMMARY OF THE COST OF THE PARK

	£	s.	d.
Quarry rights	1,000	0	0
Wages and superintendence	5,599	19	4
Lodges, walls, gateways, and conservatories	4,144	1	3
Rails, gates, and other iron work	1,080	8	2
Painting lodges, rails, &c.	154	8	10
Plants	808	3	8
Tools, sheds, and sundries	443	9	1

| | £13,230 | 10 | 4 |

17th Nov. 1881"

Lancaster Gazette clip 26 November 1881,
showing the main costs of creating the park.

The largest cost involved was that of wages, showing how labour intensive the work had been, bearing in mind that all the remodelling of the Moor land would have been done by pick and shovel.

The Mayor, Samuel Harris, described Mr Williamson as 'a gentleman who did not like show, and who shrunk from receiving any public thanks whatever in the matter'.

Alderman Greg proposed a vote of thanks, describing the park as a gift which was of the highest value to all inhabitants of the town – to the poor and to the sick, and more especially perhaps to the poor – for men who worked from morning till night but with little recreation or pleasure had now a place where they could appear in their best clothes and enjoy themselves and see their friends.

He went on to say, 'The taste displayed in laying out the moor, whilst happily preserving many of the natural features of the ground, with the facilities afforded by such a site for the enjoyment of the panoramic scenery of the district, have combined to provide for the inhabitants of Lancaster a public park which is almost unequalled for its attractiveness.'

The *Lancaster Guardian*'s report at the time (3 December 1881) gave a detailed description of the layout of the park, but described it as a partly-finished work. There were several important features mentioned, such as a summerhouse, the great plateau, the waterfall, the lake and the rustic bridge (later replaced). The summerhouse mentioned is not the present Butterfly House, as this was built *c*.1907.

> The Park comprises the whole block of quarry workings on the moor formerly known as 'Hard Times'. It divides itself into two great divisions, northern and southern, the point of division being the high-level plateau in the centre. It is now a succession of vistas of beautiful park scenery, through which smooth gravel walks pass in every direction. The paths are bordered with a fringe of grass, and from this border extend shrubberies in which every conceivable green and foliage plant proper for the purpose finds a place. The surfaces of the old hills and mounds have been smoothed and faced with green sod at their bases, the upper portions beings planted with firs and laurel.

The report continued:

> An excellent view of the Park ... is to be got from the little plateau upon which the old iron seat, placed in that spot years ago is still fixed. At the top of the first reach of the carriage drive is a large and handsome summer-house, seated to accommodate a good number of people. Keeping

along the main road you come to the great Plateau, made as level as possible, and carpeted with fresh green sods. A number of seats are fixed here, and from the elevation of the spot an immense panorama of river, landscape, sea, and mountain scenery can be viewed.

Past the Plateau the great road winds downward past a great smooth hollow … and from this spot also you can see the waterfall plashing over the brow of the highest cliff in the Park. Following the sweep of the main road you quickly come in sight of the lake, which lies at the base of a succession of great rocky cliffs. Seats are placed so that visitors can view the lake from a point of considerable height above it. The waterfall comes down the face of a cliff 80 feet in height, and is received below in a great circular basin,

An early view of the park before the Memorial was constructed (the rustic bridge still being in situ)

'Ryelands Scar' illustration by Charles Haworth for Johnson's book *Pictorial Guide to Valley of Lune*, showing the waterfall

from which the water passes by an overflow charmingly constructed into the principal body of water. From the by-path nearest the Asylum wall a second narrow path runs and conducts you to a beautiful rustic bridge [see illustration on p 75] which spans the lake at the turn.

This early illustration of the park shows the 'sliding' rock next to the Lake, which many Lancastrians have slid down as children. The scenery at this time is remarkably bare of vegetation.

An illuminated manuscript

Early the following year, the Corporation had a 'resolution of thanks' made to Mr Williamson on the handing over of the park to them in November 1881. This was illuminated on vellum, presumably because they wanted to mark the occasion somehow and demonstrate their thanks formally. The work was carried out by Mr R. Johnson, illuminator, of

Prescot Road, Old Swan, Liverpool, formerly of Lancaster. It was very well-described as follows:

> It occupies two sheets which face each other in book form. In the top left-hand corner of the first page is Mr Williamson's coat of arms, similar to that on the park gates, interwoven with and forms the initial letter of the words 'Williamson Park', and in a ribbon underneath is the motto 'nurus cereus conscientia sana'. At the bottom left-hand corner are the borough arms, and across the bottom of the page a view in the park showing the lake, the rustic foot-bridge, and the Golgotha entrance, with Ripley's Hospital and the Barracks in the distance. The opposite page is treated in much the same manner, with coats of arms on a smaller scale. At the bottom is the seal of the borough, and the signature of the Mayor, Samuel J Harris. The vellum is elegantly mounted in red morocco, richly gilt, and on the back is Mr Williamson's monogram, J.W. (*Lancaster Gazette* 4 January 1882)

The document was presented by the Committee to Mr Williamson at his house, Ryelands, after which he entertained them to dinner (*Lancaster Gazette* 14 January 1882).

Six years after the illuminated document was presented to James Williamson, he finally handed over the management of the park to the Corporation (*Lancaster Gazette* 30 June 1888). He had until then paid all the costs of improvements and repairs, and proposed to hand over an endowment fund of just under £13,000 to meet the cost of future maintenance. Now that the Corporation had the management of the park in their own hands, they had the power to draw up bye-laws for the regulation of 'vehicular traffic'. It was mentioned that 'to admit wagonettes without restriction is undesirable; they would cut up the main road through the Park, and seriously interfere with the comfort of pedestrians'.

Until this point James Williamson had been the Chairman of the Park Committee. To replace him, Mr Thomas P. Greene was appointed Chairman (*Lancaster Guardian* 23 October 1889). He was a gardener by profession, then retired, aged only 41, and living on Aldcliffe Road. It was reported that under his management the park was being well-maintained, and he was praised for the flowers he had chosen, and how beautifully they were arranged. He was due for re-election as a councillor for John O'Gaunt ward and it was felt that 'Even if Mr Greene did no other work in the Corporation except look after the Park – for that alone they ought to keep him in the Council.'

In August 1888 the Council discussed whether or not steps should be taken to place a permanent memorial in the form of a statue of the late Mr Williamson in the park, as there seemed to be some public support for this idea in the town (*Lancaster Gazette* 4 August 1888). The Mayor referred the matter back to the Committee, but it is not clear why this suggestion was never progressed.

Stealing flowers in the park

Stealing flowers from the park seemed to be a frequent occurrence and two examples are given here.

"Stealing Flowers in the Park – Two boys named William Findley, and John Briscoe, were found stealing flowers in the Williamson Park a few days ago. They were taken before the Park Committee and severely reprimanded. It is absolutely necessary that the flowers in the Park should be protected, and future offenders will not be so leniently dealt with."

Clipping from *Lancaster Gazette* dated 25 April 1885

Septimus Brown – Flower Thief

In 1890 the *Lancaster Gazette* reported the sorry tale of Septimus Brown, an 18-year-old 'table baize labourer' from Parker Street, who was found guilty of stealing part of a rose tree (*Lancaster Gazette* 26 July 1890). He was to be made an example of by the Park Committee, who for some time 'had been very much annoyed by people who went into the Park not being satisfied with looking at its beauty, but who were also in the habit of breaking down trees and carrying portions of them away'. He was therefore brought before the Judge, who said he could have imposed a fine of up to £5 or even a sentence of imprisonment, but instead fined him just 2*s*. 6*d*. with 1*s*. damages.

The Williamson Park Band

As early as 1881 the park had its own brass band playing every Saturday. The *Lancaster Gazette* (24 September 1881) reported that 'owing to the unpleasant state of the weather the Williamson Park Brass Band were obliged to curtail their programme. Visitors were numerous during the day, as through an oversight the time was not specified when the band would be in attendance'. A list of pieces that would be played the following Saturday, weather allowing, was to include: The Pirates of Penzance, Fairy Revels, Moonlit Eve and True Love, among others. Performances took place in one of the dells, as the bandstand was not built until much later. It was unfortunately removed some time in the late 1950s at the same time as the Greg Observatory was demolished.

An early Band performance in the park (Lancaster City Museums LANLM.1996.45.43)

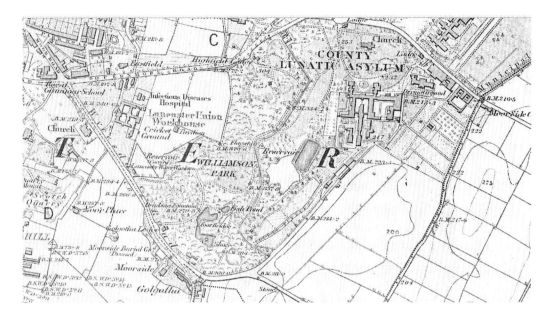

Williamson Park in 1891 from 6-inch Ordnance Survey map

Williamson Park in 1891

By 1891 the park was well-laid out, with footpaths winding across it, as shown on the 6-inch Ordnance Survey map. Many of the features we are familiar with today were not yet in existence. The lake was there with the wooden footbridge, interestingly with a 'fish pond' marked adjacent to it, approximately where the Temple Shelter is today. The fishpond was still in existence in around 1909, as the postcard showing the fishpond has the new stone bridge in the background. The quarries were no longer in evidence and abundant planting appeared to have

The old rustic footbridge which is marked on the 1891 map, and was replaced with the present stone bridge in c.1905

View in Williamson Park, Lancaster

taken their place. Two other features marked on this map were a drinking fountain and a flagstaff.

The stone plinth for the drinking fountain is still present today not far from the side of the lake. The fountain itself was made of cast iron and was made by the Sun Foundry of Glasgow (memorial drinking fountains. wordpress.com). It was of an ornate design with a domed canopy. The basin of the fountain contained the statue of a cherub with an urn.

Water was dispensed via the urn with a cup suspended on a chain. At ground level a small trough supplied water for dogs.

The fountain was unfortunately removed in 1942 as part of the war effort (see section on the park in the wars) and the *Lancaster Guardian*'s columnist, who was obviously not a fan of the fountain, reported that 'Someone with admirable courage has gone so far as to order the removal of that far from picturesque iron drinking fountain which used to flaunt its ultra Victorian facade upon the verge of the lovely lake.' This comment illustrates very well how tastes change over time.

The ornate drinking fountain next to the lake, with the rustic footbridge in the background (Lancaster City Museums LANLM.1986.23)

Winters in Victorian times were significantly harsher than the present day, and it seems that skating in the park was a regular occurrence (https://www.netweather.tv/weather-forecasts/uk/winter/winter-history).

"SKATING IN THE PARK.

Mr. Greene, in moving the confirmation of the minutes of the Park Committee, said that now winter was approaching they had instructed the Park keepers in the event of frost, to keep everybody off the pond till it was fit for skating upon, and parties would not be allowed to try it with stones or sticks as they had been in the habit of doing, and so spoiling the ice for skating. One portion would also be set apart for boys to slide upon, and they would not be allowed to make slides on that portion set apart for skating. – Mr Beesley seconded and the minutes were confirmed."

Lancaster Gazette clip 30 November 1889

Postcard view of the Lake showing the fishpond high above it (Lancaster City Museums)

THE LAKES, WILLIAMSON PARK, LANCASTER.

E 02396

The park was never formally opened, but on 24 March 1896 the Duke and Duchess of York (later King George V and Queen Mary) visited Lancaster to open the newly built Lancaster Infirmary, afterwards driving through the town in their carriage. Part of the route involved driving along the carriage road through the park and 'thus added the one thing needful to complete the consecration of this noble gift to the people of Lancaster' (*An illustrated booklet about the Williamson Park, Lancaster,* Thomas Johnson, *c.*1900).

The Greg Observatory

On one of the mounds lying to the west of the Ashton Memorial are the foundations of the Greg Observatory, named after John Greg, one of Lancaster's cotton mill owners. He had an interest in astronomy and set up his own observatory containing a large 7 ½-inch achromatic telescope in the grounds of his house at Escowbeck in Caton village. When he died in 1882, his son Albert offered the telescope as a gift to Lancaster Corporation.

However, as seemed to be the norm for the Corporation, they were in no hurry to organise a suitable site to house this gift and did not decide upon a place for it in the park until 1889. Other sites which had been under consideration were the Giant Axe Field behind the train station and the 'Oval' in Dalton Square – at that time, the statue of Queen Victoria now situated in the square did not exist. A plan for the observatory building was then prepared and it was officially opened in 1892.

As well as the large telescope, the observatory housed 'a perfect and beautiful transit instrument with an object-glass 2 3/4 inches in diameter, large enough to observe the transit of the brighter stars across the meridian in broad daylight' (from *An illustrated booklet about Williamson Park* by T. Johnson). Both these telescopes were manufactured by Thomas Cooke of York, a well-known manufacturer of telescopes in the nineteenth

DID YOU KNOW?

An astronomical clock or horologium, is a clock with special mechanisms and dials to display astronomical information, such as the relative positions of the sun, moon, zodiacal constellations and major planets.

century, and were donated by Greg's son, Albert. Smaller telescopes and an astronomical clock were among the other instruments available to visitors. The Corporation also established a weather station at the Observatory which included a standard barometer, various types of thermometer, a sunshine recorder, and a self-recording rain gauge or pluviograph.

One of the rooms contained a collection of curios, including a Zulu spear and shield and a stuffed snake, as well as prints and photographs of local scenery. Binoculars were available for visitors to view the scenery, as in those days the building was not surrounded by trees and there was a good view of Morecambe Bay. Visitors were charged one penny to enter the observatory and the first curator of the observatory, George Ingall, was allowed to keep the entrance charges as he was not paid a salary.

The Observatory's first curator, Mr George Ingall

Thomas Johnson, the writer of the booklet about the park published in 1896, described Mr Ingall as a man

> whose leisure and refined tastes admirably fit him for the post. His genial explanations of the scenery, and humorous remarks on men and manners, together with a rich fund of anecdotes collected and stored during a long and active life in the county town of Lancaster, add in no small degree to the immense popularity of the Greg Observatory.

George Ingall's life was indeed varied. He was the son of George and Jane Ingall who lived on Damside Street in Lancaster, George being a grocer by trade. Sadly, George Senior died in 1843 when George Junior was only 11 years old. By the age of 18 he was working as an upholsterer and the family were living on St Leonardgate, his mother now running the grocery business. Ten years later he was a boarder at Summer Hill House near Ulverston, an impressive country house, at the time the home of a James Clark of London and his family. Mr Clark was a magistrate and deputy lieutenant (a local official) and was obviously a man of means, as they had six house servants. George Ingall was listed as being a cabinet maker as this point, but he was not the only cabinet maker staying at the house, as 70-year-old William Hardy was also listed as boarding there, and we can only assume that the men had been employed by Mr Clark to make and install some impressive piece of furniture at the house.

George carried on working as an upholsterer until after his mother's death in 1881, when we find that he had an interesting change in occupation, possibly because his new job included accommodation. Surprisingly, he was now house steward to Eleanor Williamson at Parkfield House on Greaves Road in Lancaster! She was the wife of James Williamson Snr, the man who first provided the money to convert Lancaster Moor into a park just prior to the time that George Ingall was working for his wife. James and Eleanor had bought Parkfield House in 1871, but James had died in in 1879. A house steward was an important role in Victorian households, being similar to that of a housekeeper, and he would have been in close contact with the Williamson family, mother and son, James Williamson Jnr. This contact would obviously have stood him in good stead for being appointed curator some ten years later on the opening of the Observatory in the park.

George must have done well whilst working for the Williamson family, as he was able to retire to a new house on Derwent Road by 1891, situated high above the centre of town with a lovely view over Morecambe Bay. This location was also handy for the park.

George's appointment as curator did not go without some drama – he must have been 'brought to book' for using a gas stove within the Observatory, as in 1904 he handed in his notice, then weeks later asked for his post back. The Corporation agreed to this as long as 'the use of his gas stove be not permitted in the future'. The Observatory also employed a meteorological attendant for its small weather station situated close by, a Mr W. H. Harris being appointed to this role later on in 1904 after the previous postholder and found another appointment. George died in 1906 at the age of 73, the post of curator being advertised the year before.

James Dowbiggin: the second curator of the Observatory

In 1905 at the age of 46, James Dowbiggin was successful in his application for the post of curator (there were two other applicants). He had some experience of using the telescopes whilst they were still in Greg's home observatory (*Lancaster's Lost Observatory – A relic of Lancaster's Cotton Industry* by Peter Wade). The Corporation now promised a grand salary of 10*s*., which does not seem sufficient to run a home. James's two sons were still living at home, the eldest working as a bookkeeper at a cotton mill and the youngest as an apprentice pharmacist, so at least there was some extra money coming into the household.

James Dowbiggin was born in the parish of Quernmore in 1858, the son of George and Margaret Dowbiggin. George was a farm bailiff and the family lived at Pilgrim's Rest, Caton (Caton village was in Quernmore parish), which were farm cottages on the Gresgarth Hall estate (then known as Grassyards). By 1881 James was 22 and working as a wood sawyer. He was living with his uncle Thomas Dowbiggin at Hollinhead Farm, just further up the lane from Pilgrim's Rest Cottages. There was a bobbin manufacturer at Forge Mill close to the Gresgarth Hall estate, run by Messrs Brocklebank and Sons and, according to James Dowbiggin's obituary in the *Lancaster Guardian* (19 February 1943), he was employed by them for a time. There was also a wood mill in Caton called Rumble Row Mill (*Caton – Past and Present*). As this was also part of Gresgarth Hall estate it is possible that James worked here for a time – the mill was leased by a Mr Henry Wright who came from Manchester in about 1880 to set up as a furniture manufacturer. By the time of the 1891 census James had married Ann Alice and set up home at a house called Borwicks, very close to the sawmill, and was still working as a sawyer. It must have been whilst living in Caton that he visited the observatory at Escowbeck House, the home of John Greg.

Something must have occurred at this point to force a change in James's life, as by the time of the 1901 census, prior to his appointment at the Observatory, James was working as a 'librarian overseer' at the Amicable Society, the forerunner of the free public library movement, and had moved his family to Willow Lane in Lancaster. The Amicable Society was situated on Church Street and by the time of the 1911 census he had moved to 5 New Road in the centre of town, on the corner of Church Street.

In 1905 when James Dowbiggin was appointed to the Observatory, the Ashton Memorial was not yet built, and the balcony of the Observatory was used as an observation post by visitors wishing to view the scenery visible from the park. His obituary states that to give travellers coming from afar something to do on dull days 'he began collecting interesting curios and commenced by purchasing a few antiques and gradually by gifts got together a most interesting collection'. However, as previously mentioned, we know that there was already a collection of curios at the

Photo of James Dowbiggin stood outside the Observatory (Courtesy of Lancashire County Council's Red Rose Collections)

Observatory which had been assembled by George Ingall, but perhaps he had removed these on his retirement.

James Dowbiggin was also a member of the Lancaster Astronomical and Scientific Society and later became their Honourable Meteorologist. Weather readings from the meteorological station had been taken daily from the time it was opened and weather reports were displayed at the Observatory itself and also at the Storey Institute on Meeting House Lane. When the new Town Hall opened in 1909 on Dalton Square, the reports were also posted on a notice board on the side of the old Town Hall buildings on the New Street side, just round the corner from James's home on New Road. Eventually James became the President of the Astronomical and Scientific Society and so was obviously very well-regarded in these circles – quite an achievement for a simple wood sawyer!

The decline of the 'lost observatory'

In 1923 the Observatory building was noted to be in a bad state of repair and necessary work, including painting, was carried out. An episode of vandalism in 1929 caused damage to one of the meteorological instruments, a solar maximum thermometer, and also to the roof of the building. The roof had been damaged by the throwing of stones at the bell on the roof on a day when there was a half-day holiday from school. This was a bell which had been donated by a Councillor Seward in 1909, the aim being for the bell to be rung to announce closing time in the park. The bell had been cast in Lancaster in 1794 by one of the councillor's ancestors, Mr Abram Seward.

In October 1937 it was noted that the Observatory was now used almost exclusively as a meteorological station (*Lancaster Gazette* 29 October 1937). Mr Dowbiggin was now in his late 70s and the monthly weather reports published in the *Lancaster Guardian* were being compiled by the Clerk to the Observatory, Mr Neville Holden, who was also the Coroner.

In October 1939 it was reported that four boys aged between 14 and 16 had broken into the Observatory through a window and stolen a bayonet belonging to Mr Dowbiggin, together with ten lenses, a thermometer and two measuring glasses. This nicely illustrates the fact that Mr Dowbiggin had an eclectic collection of items on display at the Observatory. The boys claimed that the bayonet had been first buried in the park, then dug up, and they threw it in some rushes on the Marsh – a likely tale. The boys were put under the care of a probation officer for their crimes.

James Dowbiggin retired on 31 July 1939 at the age of 80, on a retirement allowance of £1 per week. It was also in this year that the weather station failed its Air Ministry inspection. Lancaster Corporation decided not to replace James and handed the use of the Observatory over to Lancaster Grammar School. The Corporation agreed to maintain the fabric of the building, but the outbreak of the War meant that priorities lay elsewhere, and damp eventually caused problems with the equipment. The estimated cost of repairing these items to working condition was considered to be too high and the school's headmaster ordered the boys to stop using the building in 1944.

Thereafter it seems that the weather and vandalism took their toll, and the building was demolished in the late 1950s, together with the Bandstand. It is thought that the telescope was not destroyed, but was

Greg Observatory (Lancaster City Museums LANLM.1996.45.327)

THE OBSERVATORY, WILLIAMSON PARK, LANCASTER.

moved to a radar station in Derby (*Lancaster Guardian* 31 March 1995). Nowadays the foundations are all that remain, and these can be found on the top of the knoll just to the west of the Memorial.

The trams ran from 1903 until sometime in the 1920s, beginning in the centre of town at Dalton Square and running along South Road, up Bowerham Road and Coulston Road and terminating at the Wyresdale Road entrance. A separate line ran southwards from South Road to Scotforth. The service was never really financially viable and so was discontinued (www.tramwaybadgesandbuttons.com).

All that is left standing of the Observatory (Lancaster City Museums LANLM.1983.13.2)

ESIDE WILLIAMSON PARK, LANCASTER.

Old postcards showing Edwardian visitors enjoying the Park and the area that is now the Friends' garden (Lancaster City Museums LANLM.1996.45.607 and LANLM.1998.56.5)

FLOWER BEDS, WILLIAMSON PARK, LANCASTER.

Old postcard showing the fountain soon after installation in the early 1900s
(Lancaster City Museums LANLM.1996.45.613)

The updating of the park in the early twentieth century

A second round of works initiated by James Williamson, now Lord Ashton, began in around 1905. The rustic footbridge was replaced with one constructed out of stone, as were the park shelters. Other features were added, including the Temple Shelter, a Bandstand, the Palm House (now the Butterfly House), a fountain for the lake, new roads and paths and a spanned roof greenhouse (i.e., with an apex roof as opposed to a lean-to type).

The construction of the Ashton Memorial

The most notable feature added at this time was the Ashton Memorial, known as the 'Park Structure' when first under construction (*Ledger Book for Ashton Memorial*, Lancashire Archives), sometimes called the 'Structure' by locals today. Lord Ashton originally intended to dedicate this building to the memory of his second wife, Jessie, who had died in 1904, the year before construction began ('The folly to end all follies?' Andrew White, *The Follies Journal*, 2006). However, he soon acquired a third wife, Florence Maud, whom he married in 1909. This was also the year the Memorial was completed, and so the dedication slab inside reads instead 'This building was erected by the Right Hon. Lord Ashton as a memorial to his family and presented to the inhabitants of Lancaster' and was backdated to 1907.

The Memorial was constructed at the highest point in the park, on an area sometimes known as the 'sixpence' due to its small size. Lord Ashton had originally planned this to be the site of the statue of Queen Victoria,

The new stone footbridge showing the observatory on the skyline
(Lancaster City Museums 2250)

now situated in Dalton Square, but changed his mind in 1904, telling the
Corporation that he now had 'a view to the utilisation of the site in the
Park for another purpose' (*Corporation Minute Books*).

Architect John Belcher

John Belcher was well into his 60s by the time he was commissioned
to design the Memorial, the Palm House and the Temple Shelter. He
was a prominent, turn of the century, London-based architect and had
previously designed many other prestigious buildings of the Victorian era,
including Colchester Town Hall, a building which is very reminiscent of
the Ashton Memorial. He was the son of an architect of the same name,
and studied architecture in Paris in the 1860s. He was in partnership with
his father until 1875 and their most notable project was the Mappin and
Webb building in the City of London, sadly demolished in 1994 to make
way for '1 Poultry'.

He was a member of the Royal Academy of Art and was a founder
of the Edwardian Baroque style, of which the Ashton Memorial is an
example. Fortunately for us, our John Belcher building still stands.

Colchester Town Hall, designed by John
Belcher in 1898, in the same Baroque style as
the Ashton Memorial

Plan of west elevation of Memorial
(Lancaster City Museums)

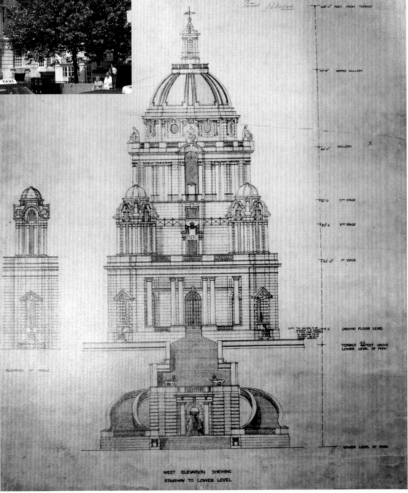

Construction of Memorial c.1908
(Lancaster City Museums 2216)

The ledger book for the Memorial shows that John Belcher was paid the total sum of £3,198 2s. 5d. (about £300,000 in today's terms) in six separate payments. Waring and Gillow were paid the huge sum of £47,472 7s. 9d. (about £480,000 in today's terms) in nineteen separate payments over a period from 1906 to 1908, the last payment being listed as 'balance of contract'.

Waring and Gillow are more famously known as prestigious furniture makers, and many examples of their furniture can be seen in the Judges' Lodgings Museum, near Lancaster Castle. However, they had also diversified into general building works and were the main contractors used in the building of the Memorial. They cut the stone with new diamond saws at their stone yard in Ashton Road (A. White, 'The Folly to end all Follies?'). Various types of stone were used: Portland stone for the main elevations, Cornish granite for staircases and main steps, and Longridge grit and Hopton Wood limestone from Derbyshire in the building. The main dome is made of copper.

Mr Woodward's stone yard

There is a detailed description in the *Lancaster Guardian* around 1907 of how the stonework for the memorial (and the town hall) was cut and then constructed at the stone yard which was situated on Ashton Road. The stone yard was organised extremely efficiently by a Mr J. H. Woodward, possibly Mr Joseph Woodward, a stonemason of public works from the Wirral, who would have been in his late 60s by the time the memorial was being built. The newspaper describes his stone yard as being 'one of the half dozen largest and best equipped in the country'. The roughly quarried stone arrived at one end of the yard in railway trucks and travelled down the yard, through various 'shops', until it left the yard at the other end as finished blocks ready for fitting directly into the building, with no further working on site being required. The dimensions, shape and special character of each block were taken from the architect's drawings and laid out on paper for each workman. Approximately 300 tons of worked stone per week were prepared and sent out in the order in which they were required.

The machinery in the yard seems to have been the latest available. Electricity was generated by two 55hp suction gas engines, which were needed to operate two electric cranes, one capable of lifting ten tons and the other five, the cranes travelling on gantries from one end of the yard to the other. At that time, electricity supplies were variable and, if they existed at all, were mainly only suitable for electric lighting. There were numerous stone-cutting machines 'of the type familiar to many people, but with the latest improvements, which saw up blocks of stone as easily as baulks of timber are split up into lengths'. The diamond saws are referred to as 'special machines' and were used for cutting hard stone such as the Derbyshire limestone. They are described as circular, the largest wheel being 7 feet 4 inches (about 2.25 metres) in diameter with 170 'black Brazilian diamonds' electrically welded all round.

Mr Woodward's yard must have looked very similar to this old photo of Box stone yard

The updating of the park in the early twentieth century

Site Supervisor: George Richard Leadsom's 'Poem in Stone'

Waring and Gillow were clearly used to bringing in the best workmen to carry out key roles in such prestigious contracts, and did not use local people for the Memorial. The man who was brought in to supervise the building project was Mr George Richard Leadsom from Selly Park in Birmingham. He is listed in the 1911 census as a building manager, but he would only have been aged 30 in 1907, the year that building of the Memorial commenced.

The writer in the *Lancaster Guardian* gave a highly descriptive account of Mr Leadsom's capabilities:

> He is an artist himself, albeit a very practical one – a man who knows how to reduce art to practice, and design to reality. Under his care this beautiful 'poem in stone', the creation of Mr Belcher's artistic brain, is crystallised into shape. Whether it be a beautiful carved block of stone, a rounded column, an arm of steel ... he is *au fait* with it, and sees that it is put into the right place.

The article describes a large crane which rested on two legs, but which seemed to rest on the 'roof of the first stage'. The advanced technology shown in the stone yard was also demonstrated at the actual building site, as the crane is fitted with both telegraph and telephone apparatus so that the 'engine man can be instructed from the top when to raise or lower a block of stone'. The article also mentions that the stonework was covered with a 'special preparation' to protect it from the 'action of the atmosphere' until the building was finished, when the covering would be scraped off and the stonework washed.

The Clerk of Works: Mr T. W. Gamage

Mr Gamage only gets a very brief mention in the *Guardian* article, and is described as the architect's representative on the site and as a 'valuable assistance to the builders'. He was also from London and was probably employed by John Belcher to supervise this important project. He would have been in his 60s at the beginning of the construction and so would have brought a great deal of experience from his working life.

Herbert Hampton: sculptor

Herbert Hampton was a London sculptor of some repute. He is known to have produced a number of royal monuments and there are examples of statues of Queen Victoria by him in Ipswich, India and New Zealand, as well as the one we have in Lancaster's Dalton Square. He was commissioned to produce four sculptures for the exterior of the Ashton Memorial, representing 'Commerce', 'History', 'Science' and 'Art'. These are positioned at the level of the second viewing galleries at the base of the dome, and are therefore not easily visible.

One of Hampton's sculptures on the west side of the Memorial

He also created out some relief sculptures on the exterior lintels of the windows at the first-floor level, including a mower with his scythe, a sailing boat and a railway locomotive.

George Murray: artist

Murray was born in 1875 in the Scottish town of Blairgowrie, the son of a cabinet maker. He was an artist and designer and specialised in decorative painting and mosaics. He also painted landscapes in Scotland, Italy and Spain, and trained at the Royal College of Art. He was one of the group of artists called the 'Blairgowrie Boys', centred around William Geddes and his son Ewan, who made the town a popular place for artists to settle at the time. Murray painted four large canvasses for the ceiling of the lower dome of the Memorial representing similar themes to those of Hampton's sculptures: Commerce, History, Art and Science. He was living in London in 1911, in common with others who worked on the Memorial, shortly after his work there.

John Summerfield: manager at Anthony Bell & Sons Marble Works

John Summerfield played a prominent part in the marble and mosaic work in the Ashton Memorial, and also in the Town Hall (*Lancaster Guardian* 11 January 1946). He was originally from Staffordshire but at the time of the 1911 census he was living at 37 Kirkes Road in Lancaster. He was the manager at Anthony Bell & Sons Marble Works which was situated at 32 Parliament Street in Lancaster. This Grade II listed building is now an Indian restaurant. Mr Summerfield died in 1946 at the age of 82.

The former marble works building on Parliament Street

Walter Gilbert: sculptor, designer and metalworker

Walter Gilbert was responsible for the metalwork in the Memorial. He achieved international fame as a sculptor, metalworker and designer, carrying out many important schemes in this and other countries, including Buckingham Palace Gates and a war memorial in Liverpool Anglican Cathedral. He also designed the war memorial at Greaves Methodist Church (*Lancaster Guardian* 25 January 1946). He was born in Rugby, but lived in North Bromsgrove, just south of Birmingham, at the time of the 1911 census. His occupation at that time was listed as iron and bronze sculptor and metalworker, plaster-worker, president of a cabinet-making company and director of a wholesale lumber company, the latter two in Canada.

He died in 1946 at the age of 75.

*

It is obvious from the kind of materials, technology and expertise described above that construction was not going to be cheap and, in spite of various cost-cutting measures, the total cost of building the Ashton Memorial was around £87,000, equivalent to approximately £8.8 million today. The savings made at the time included not building in solid stone as originally intended, instead using a steel frame and concrete with stone cladding. The concrete contained a high proportion of fly-ash, a waste product from mill engines. Unfortunately, these cost-cutting measures resulted in problems with the structure of the Memorial at various times over the decades, as will be seen later. The Memorial was opened to the public without ceremony in October 1909. The *Lancashire Evening Post*, mindful of the possibility of the actions of vandals, reported that it was 'hoped they would not mark or disfigure in any way the beautiful building'.

Palm House c.1905 (Lancaster City Museums LANLM.1996.45.329)

The Palm House

The Palm House was also designed by John Belcher. It was completed two years before the Memorial and was opened to the public in July 1907. The entries in the ledger for the building of the Palm House begin several months before those of the Memorial, and so it seems likely that this construction was begun first. This is nicely demonstrated in the postcard below, which shows the bandstand being used for a concert with a half-constructed Memorial behind and, on the far left, the Palm House which seems to be completed. In the foreground of the early postcard view (above) can be seen evidence of wooden fencing which would have surrounded the construction site of the Memorial. The building in the far distance seen in the top left-hand corner is the newer extension to Lancaster Asylum, known as 'The Annexe' and built in 1883. It was converted into apartments known as 'The Residence' in 2016.

Items for the fountain, bandstand and temple are also listed in the ledger along with the Palm House entries. John Belcher was paid a total of

Bandstand *c*.1908 showing construction of Memorial in background
(Lancaster City Museums)

£202 4*s*. 9*d*. for the Palm House and £31 10*s*. 5*d*. for the Temple. Gillow & Co were paid £259 14*s*. for 'carving in Palm House' and £131 16*s*. 6*d*. for joinery work in the Temple.

The Palm House had a heating chamber underneath which was designed to be connected to the Memorial in order to heat both buildings. The *Lancashire Evening Post* (5 July 1907) described the interior as having palms in the centre with ferns and flowers placed around. The central palm was 18 feet high and two others were 15 feet, and the house also contained 'one of the finest Auracanias [this is probably meant to say Araucaria, better known as a monkey

DID YOU KNOW?

The company is listed in the ledger as Gillow & Co, although in 1897 the business had been acquired by S. J. Waring and Sons, a London-based company specialising in furniture and decorations, and the name was changed to Waring and Gillow.

Postcard showing Palm House Interior, posted 1908 (Lancaster City Museums
LANLM.1994.94.5)

puzzle tree] in the land'. There was also an orange tree, said to have
created much interest, bearing two crops of fruit, the ripe and the green.
The east wall (to the back of the house) was to be what we would now call
a 'living wall', being covered in moss and planted with ferns.

Unlike the Memorial, which was built under the supervision of outside
contractors, the Palm House was built by Corporation workmen under
the direct supervision of Mr Mount, who was the Borough Surveyor. It
seems that the Memorial was seen as a special project by Lord Ashton,
requiring the experience of those from the capital, but the palm house was
not.

The Bandstand and the bands

Bands were employed to play in the park even from before the building
of the bandstand, when they played in one of the dells or on top of the
'sixpence' (the small area of land where the Memorial was eventually built).

In 1904 the *Minute Books* of the Council stated that pieces to be played were 'to be of a bright nature, and not too long, and the intervals between each piece not to exceed five minutes'. Bands were paid £5 for each two-hour performance, each band to have not less than 24 performers. Three different bands played on different days, the King's Own Depot, the Borough Band and the Rifle Volunteer Band. During the building of the 'Structure' in 1906, performances were given on the Giant Axe football ground.

During World War I the band of the King's Own Depot played, and during the 1920s the *Lancaster Guardian* reported that thousands of people enjoyed the Sunday concerts. Some of the bands playing in the park at this time included again the King's Own, plus the Standfast Works Band and the Lancaster Discharged Soldiers' Military Band. In the 1930s chairs were purchased for hire at band concerts in the park, the charge being 2*d*. per chair for each performance, and in 1938 it was thought necessary to ask the Chief Constable to supply special constables to be on duty to control the audience during band performances!

It seems that the days of the Bandstand in the park were numbered when in 1948 the *Lancaster Guardian* reported that 'it is impossible to hear the music unless one happens to be in a very advantageous position',

Lancaster Borough Band 1905 (IBEW.org.uk)

Standfast Works Band at the foot of the Ashton Memorial (Lancaster City Museums LANLM.2003.38)

even on occasions when the weather was 'favourable'. The Council, in particular Alderman Mrs Musgrave-Hoyle, undertook to find a fresh location, although I can find no further mention of this. We know that the Bandstand was still in use as late as 1955, as the King's Own Royal Regiment (TA) gave a concert, although it was stated that the high wind sometimes blew over the music stands! The *Guardian* reported that the programme included 'the overture "Morning, Noon and Night" by Suppé and a selection from the Gilbert & Sullivan comic opera "Iolanthe."' With hindsight, the top of a hill was probably not the best choice of location, however grand it looked, and it would have been better placed in one of the sheltered dells.

DID YOU KNOW?

Franz von Suppé (1819–95) was an Austrian composer of light operas and other theatre music.

The park's gardeners

The first gardeners: Richard Thornton and Thomas Leeming

The design and initial laying out of the park gardens was carried out by landscape architect John Maclean of Castle Donington. He was assisted by Peter Shieldon, 'public park gardener', who, in the 1881 census, resided at Williamson Park Lodge, Golgotha, and John Smart, a landscape gardener originally from Coventry. However, by the time of the 1891 census their roles had been taken over by Richard Thornton, gardener, living at the Wyresdale Road Lodge, and Thomas Leeming, gardener, living at the Quernmore Road Lodge.

By 1901 Thomas had moved on and was living on Aldrens Lane, over the river in Skerton, although he was still working as a gardener, possibly at Ryelands Park, and was still employed by the Corporation as he was allowed a one shilling per week wage rise in 1913. Richard had been promoted to Park Superintendent and was still living at the Wyresdale Road Lodge. This Lodge was convenient for the greenhouses which were situated where the car park is now sited. Joseph Dearden, gardener, was living at the Quernmore Road Lodge.

Richard Thornton died on 6 July 1910 at the age of 55. The Park Committee did not treat his grieving widow, Mary Ann, very kindly, as only nine days after Richard's death the Park Committee agreed to give her just a further two weeks to remain living in the Lodge. They did allow her to treat the vegetables in the Lodge garden as her property, however. The council minutes note that Mrs Thornton had applied for a pension from the Corporation, but the Committee 'decided to do nothing in the matter'. She went on to live at 11 Hartington Street in a tiny terraced house with her adult niece who worked as a cotton weaver, and who presumably did her best to keep a roof over her aunt's head.

Thomas Townson, Deputy Head Gardener, 1899–1934

In 1911 Thomas Townson, gardener, was living at the Quernmore Road Lodge. An article in the *Lancaster Guardian* reported his son Henry's memories of living in the park. Henry was born in Quernmore Road Lodge and his father was second-in-charge of the gardens until his retirement in 1934 after 35 years of service. Henry remembers that his father tended nineteen flowerbeds outside the Palm House. Every year he planted beds at the bottom of the Memorial into a display emulating the crown, each flower being carefully chosen to match the colour of the different jewels. He was well paid, earning £3 12*s.* 6*d.* per week, but there were nine members of the family to feed. Henry remembers that there were ten gardeners employed to work in the park and that the head gardener did indeed live in the Wyresdale Road Lodge, adjacent to the greenhouses. As a boy he also used to go into the Observatory to stargaze but, not surprisingly, the curator, Mr Dowbiggin, would not allow them to play in the building (*Lancaster Guardian* 31 March 1995).

Joseph Dearden: Head Gardener 1910–39 'A life measured in trees'

In 1910, after the death of Richard Thornton, Joseph Dearden was promoted to Head Gardener and he was given a wage increase from 27*s.* to 33*s.* per week, plus accommodation in the Wyresdale Road Lodge. The death of the Head Gardener resulted in a wave of promotions and wage increases: Thomas Townson 24*s.* to 25*s.* per week with accommodation in the Quernmore Road Lodge; Mr Sandham 24*s.* to 26*s.* per week; and Mr Strickland 23*s.* to 24*s.* per week. At this point it was also agreed to employ another gardener at a wage of 22*s.* per week. By 1913 there was a total of eight gardeners employed at Williamson Park, six of them living in their own accommodation outside the park gates.

Joseph Dearden's career was summed up in an article in the *Lancaster*

Thomas Townson, deputy head gardener, in the garden of his lodge in the park (Courtesy of his family)

Guardian on his retirement in 1938. He was Head Gardener at Williamson Park for 29 years, beginning his career as an apprentice gardener under Richard Thornton in 1895. During his time as Head Gardener the number of staff employed in the park grew from six to twelve and the number of greenhouses doubled from two to four, indicating the growth of the work carried out by the park's department. The number of bedding-out plants cultivated in the greenhouses had grown seven-fold to 70,000, including 3,000 geraniums and 6,000 antirrhinums. However, Mr Dearden's favourite flowers were chrysanthemums, which were used to decorate the Town Hall for special occasions, including for royal visits. A rainy chrysanthemum show day was the cause of his only period of sickness in all his working life, as he contracted muscular rheumatism.

The *Lancaster Guardian* concluded that 'Mr Dearden's life is not measured by years, but trees. When he started work at Williamson Park he was able to trim many of the trees without the aid of a ladder. Now he uses ladders 30 and 40 feet long, and the evergreen trees have to be kept down to that height by annual lopping' (*Lancaster Guardian* 27 May 1938).

James Smith: wartime Park Superintendent with royal credentials, 1938–43

The post of Park Superintendent had been created by the Parks Committee in 1938 after the death of Head Gardener Joseph Dearden, and the new role included responsibility for Ryelands Park, Lune Bank Gardens and Dallas Road Gardens, in addition to Williamson Park. Although born in Perthshire, James Smith grew up in Leeds where his father, Mr D. Smith, had been Horticultural Superintendent to the Leeds Education Authority for 26 years.

James came to Lancaster with an excellent pedigree in gardening. He began his horticultural career at the age of 16 when he spent four years working at Harewood House Gardens, just north of Leeds, the home of the then Princess Royal, Mary, who was the only daughter of George V. Harewood House has over 100 acres of gardens which were laid out by Lancelot 'Capability' Brown in the 1760s. This time would have been spent serving his 'apprenticeship', learning how to care for a large country house garden on the job. He must have been well thought of as his next move was to the Royal Gardens at Windsor where he spent over two years, followed by a studentship at Kew Gardens. From there he obtained a post as Supervising Foreman in the Manchester Parks Department and then as Deputy Parks Superintendent at Hayes and Harlington in Middlesex. From there he came to Lancaster as the youngest Park Superintendent in the country at the age of only 29.

The Second World War began only twelve months after James took up his role in Lancaster, but before that the *Lancaster Guardian* reported (12 February 1943) that 'In that short time he stimulated the Corporation's gardening staff to a pitch of enthusiastic emulation that would have considerably enhanced the sylvan and floral attractions of the City.'

The outbreak of the war meant that food production became a priority and the hot-houses at both Williamson Park and Ryelands Park were used to grow vegetable seedlings. These were needed for growing on in over 50 acres of land, principally at Ryelands and Greaves, although the flower beds in front of the Ashton Memorial were also turned over to the production of vegetables. Demonstration allotments were laid out at both Ryelands and Williamson Parks in order to help those who were not accustomed to growing their own produce, and seedlings at economic prices were also made available to allotment holders.

"<u>City of Lancaster.</u>
<u>Parks Department.</u>
<u>Vegetable Seedling</u>
<u>Distribution Scheme</u>

In connection with the above scheme, the Parks Department are offering limited quantities of early cabbage and cauliflower, celery and parsley for immediate planting.
Unlimited quantities of Maincrop and Winter Greens of all kinds will be available from the end of May onwards at a cost of 4d per score and may be obtained from the Park Superintendent at the Nursery centres – Williamson Park, Ryelands Park and Greaves House Gardens. Persons who have placed orders for other materials are requested to collect at an early date

FREDERICK HILL,

City Engineer and Surveyor.
Town Hall, Lancaster.
14th May 1941"

Clipping from *Lancaster Guardian* 23 May 1941

James Smith had a policy of retaining some of the floral features at both Ryelands and Williamson parks and the *Guardian* described this as a wise policy and commented that 'It was refreshing to the eye and a relief to the mind, and certainly contributed to the strengthening of the citizens' morale'. He was described as being 'ever ready to offer helpful advice and assistance to all amateur horticulturalists and allotment-holders'. This was demonstrated by the fact that he was Show Secretary for the Lancaster Horticultural and Allotment Holders' Association and delivered a series of instructive lectures to their members and the public under the auspices of the City Education Committee. Another innovation was the setting up of notice boards at the parks giving valuable information in relation to the sowing and rotation of crops and methods of dealing with pests.

James also oversaw the event of the ceremonial 'planting of the City Council'. This unusual idea was the brainchild of the Chairman of the Parks Committee, Mrs H. L. Musgrave-Hoyle, and involved the planting of trees and shrubs laid out in the exact form of seating in the City Council Chamber. Each shrub or tree was labelled with the name of the individual represented and the scheme was planted out on the slopes to the south of the Memorial.

James's time at Lancaster only came to an end when he obtained a post as Parks and Gardens Superintendent and Borough Meteorologist at Cheltenham Spa in 1943. The *Guardian* tells us that his starting salary was £500 with free residence and car allowance.

DID YOU KNOW?

Mrs Hermione Musgrave-Hoyle was Mayor of Lancaster in 1938/39, the second female to have the position. She lived at Croftlands in Caton. She died in 1961 at the age of 71.

Williamson Park during the First World War

There was a general shortage of male labour during the First World War, and in the case of Williamson Park this was evidenced in August 1915 by a request to the Corporation from Mr Windham Hale, who was Honourable Secretary of the Lancashire Committee for Promoting the Employment of Women in Agriculture. He wished for permission for 'certain ladies to attend in the Park for the purpose of obtaining training in Horticulture'. It was resolved by the Parks Committee that ladies be allowed to attend 'from time to time at their own expense, not more than four being in attendance at any one time, and to act under the direction of Mr Dearden, the Park Superintendent'. However, by April 1916 only 100 agricultural vacancies had been filled across Lancashire.

In January 1916 the Military Service Act allowed for conscription of single men aged between 18 and 41, with exceptions for some such as

DID YOU KNOW?

The Lancashire Committee for Promoting the Employment of Women in Agriculture was a campaign to encourage women 'back to the land' in 1915, just after the start of the First World War. However, women were reluctant to return to the working conditions known by their grandmothers in the nineteenth century and were more tempted by the higher wages on offer in munitions factories.

clergymen, teachers and some industrial workers. Workers who wanted to be exempt from signing up had to plead their case before a tribunal. One such application from a plant-grower employed at Williamson Park was made to Lancaster's Tribunal in May 1916 and his case was supported by the Corporation on the grounds of his expert knowledge. However, the Chairman of the Tribunal pointed out that 'the planting of trees in the park was not of national importance. If potatoes were being planted in the park for the feeding of the people it might be considered to be in the national interest'. Unfortunately for him, his application was refused, and it can be assumed that he was conscripted.

At the end of World War I, part of Lancaster's plan to observe the Peace Celebrations was to floodlight the Memorial, and local advertisers took the opportunity to offer customers fireworks, crackers, flags and bunting (*Lancaster Guardian* 2 November 1945). It is unclear whether the floodlighting plans came to fruition, but this is the first mention found of what is now a common occurrence showing the landmark off to its very best.

Williamson Park during the Second World War

'Black-Out Viewed From Park Structure – Earl Peel an Interested Spectator'

This is a headline from the *Lancaster Guardian* dated 19 May 1939. The British government had begun to prepare the civilian population for war as early as 1938, so Air Raid Wardens wanted to ensure that Lancaster would be able to properly instigate black-out conditions in the event that war would take place. There was no better place to observe the effects of the black-out than the balcony on the Ashton Memorial. The gathering on the balcony included the Chief Constable of Lancaster, William Thompson, who was the Co-ordination Officer of the ARP (Air Raid Precaution), as well as Earl Peel, who was the grandson of Lord Ashton and was also Chief Air Raid Warden for the city. The test black-out seems to have been a success as only stray lights were observed, which may have been street lamps or stationary vehicles.

A further black-out exercise was carried out in July 1939, and again those in charge wanted to view the results from the Memorial. This time the official party included the Mayor, Mrs H. L. Musgrave-Hoyle. However, when they arrived at the park the gates were locked, but the Mayor set an example of prompt action in an emergency by climbing over the high iron railings to gain admission, which caused some surprise to the others in the party (*Lancaster Guardian* 21 July 1939).

The war began on 1 September 1939 and shortly afterwards the ARP Committee recommended to the Council that in the event of an air-raid

warning being given, the caretakers of the various parks should unlock
the gates so that the general public could enter. This was thought to be
unwise as there were no shelters available in the parks, and urgent action
was required to identify shelters and to let people know where they were,
otherwise they 'would be running around scared stiff and some would be
hysterical' (*Lancashire Evening Post* 27 September 1939).

Florence Ashton rosebed

In 1940 Lady Florence Ashton, Lord Ashton's third wife, contacted Mrs
Musgrave-Hoyle in her position as Chairman of the Parks Committee
and offered to present to the Corporation a bed of 'sweet-smelling hybrid
musk roses'. This offer was gratefully accepted and on 6 June 1940 the
rose bed was formally handed over by Lady Ashton. I assume the woman
who can be seen in the picture standing to the right of Lady Ashton is
Mrs Musgrave-Hoyle,
as she was no longer
Mayor at this point.

Lady Ashton presenting
the rose bed, June 1940
(Lancaster City Museums)

Dig for Victory!

During the early part of the Second World War under the direction of James Smith, Park Superintendent, much was done to use the park to both help educate gardeners about how to successfully grow food, and also as a place to actually grow vegetables. Photographic exhibitions of vegetable growing 'illustrating all the modern arts of vegetable cultivation' were displayed at the Ashton Memorial and in the conservatory at Ryelands Park in connection with the Food Production Campaign.

As well as using some of the flower beds to grow vegetables, the park had a demonstration allotment. In Mr Smith's first annual report on the Food Production Campaign, he stated that 'During the season an area of approximately 20 acres has been cultivated and cropped with farm and garden crops, including potatoes and oats.'

Display of vegetables – 'Victory Garden Show at Ashton Hall September 1941 – Mr Stirzaker, Head Gardener at Greaves House, at Lancaster City Parks Department Stand' (Lancaster City Museums)

However, in 1941 the *Lancaster Guardian* reported both on the beauty of the park and on its successful vegetable production. It was 'a tonic calculated to help one to retain a proper perspective with regard to the problems of war-time existence' and the 'restorative effects of the masses of bloom and with the rhododendrons as a kaleidoscopic background' (13 June 1941). In August it reported that the ornamental flower beds normally flanking the Memorial contained instead scarlet stems of beet, healthy-looking dwarf beans and swedes.

There was also a Vegetable Plant Distribution Scheme allowing gardeners to order seed potatoes, tomato plants and maincrop and winter greens from the Park Superintendent. Approximately 90,000 vegetable seedlings were distributed in this way in 1941. During the severe weather in early 1945 the palms in the Palm House were killed off and instructions were given to utilise the space for the growing of tomatoes. It is possible that the Council had been unable to heat the Palm House by this point in the war.

The flower beds in the park were even used for propaganda purposes. At the foot of the Memorial was 'a spectacular and beautifully-designed flower bed in the shape of a crown. At the top was the slogan 'Lend to defend the right to be free' and in the bottom half was the clarion call coined by Herbert Morrison, the wartime Home Secretary, 'Go to it' to mobilise the population (the Morrison Shelter was also named after him). The *Lancashire Evening Post* called this a 'floral advertising board' and said that it had also previously been designed as an ARP badge to appeal for volunteers (10 July 1940).

The 'Happy Land Girls'

There was extra pressure on the remaining male gardeners after some were called up to serve in the armed forces, the staff being reduced by around fifty per cent by 1942. Eight members of the Women's Land Army were therefore recruited to help and were split into two groups, four for each park. The *Lancaster Guardian* (5 August 1942) described them as being 'attractive blondes and brunettes, all heathily tanned and vitally interested in the work in hand'. They worked a 48-hour week beginning at 7.30 each morning. Four of them were Lancaster residents: Susan

Land Army Girls in Williamson Park (Lancaster City Museums)

Land Army Girls in front of Williamson Park greenhouses (Lancaster City Museums)

Moore of York Road who had been a clerical worker; Margaret Hunter of Newsham Road, previously employed at the Lancaster and District Co-operative Society; Marjorie Bennett, also of Newsham Road, a silk warper; and Ethel Pimlott of Derwent Road who had worked for the Civil Service.

"GOOD FRIDAY.

_____

UNITED OPEN-AIR SERVICE
IN WILLIAMSON PARK
at 4 p.m.

_____

The Band of I.T.C., The King's Own Royal Regiment

(By kind permission of Lt.-Col. R.P.
White, M.C., and Officers, Band-
Master, B.H. Brown).
Will play in The Bandstand from
3.30pm and accompany the Service
THE WORSHIPFUL THE MAYOR
OF LANCASTER
will preside and an Address will be
given by
THE LORD BISHOP OF LANCASTER
and the REV. J. GOLDSBOROUGH
(Greaves Methodist Church)"

Lancaster Guardian 10 April 1941

During the war years the park was often used for open-air church services. In 1941 the service arranged by the Bishop of Lancaster for Good Friday had to be rearranged due to bad weather and was eventually held in July. At this service the Bishop gave a sermon 'stressing the fact that on the material side the war must be fought to a finish and Hitler and his gang destroyed, but the war must also be won on the spiritual plane and to do that it was not sufficient for people just to go to church for special occasions' (*Lancaster Guardian* 11 July 1941). It should be noted that the

Bishop, the Right Reverend Pollard, was also a combatant officer in the 3rd Battalion of the Home Guard.

The Council gave permission in 1942 for the Lancaster Free Church Federal Council to hold open-air services on Sundays during the summer months, as long as they did not clash with the usual Sunday services held in churches in the city. However, it was not only church services which were held in the park. In June 1942 the Lancaster branch of the Communist Party advertised open-air meetings to be held every Sunday at 3 pm at the entrance to Williamson Park.

"COMMUNIST PARTY, LANCASTER BRANCH.

OPEN AIR MEETINGS:
EVERY SATURDAY, 6.30 p.m. MARKET SQUARE.
EVERY SUNDAY, 3 p.m., WILLIAMSON'S PARK
ENTRANCE.
Questions and discussions invited.

COME AND HEAR THE COMMUNIST PARTY'S POLICY
FOR
LANCASTER – A SECOND FRONT NOW."

Lancaster Guardian 5 June 1942

DID YOU KNOW?

In 1941 when the Soviet Union was
invaded by Germany, the CPGB came
out in support of the war on the grounds
that it had now become a war between
fascism and the Soviet Union. They
launched a campaign for a Second Front
in order to support the USSR and speed
the defeat of the Axis – Italy, Germany
and Japan.

The Home Guard

The Home Guard also made use of the park during the Second World War. The Home Guard unit for Lancaster City was the 3rd Battalion, and B Company's defensive positions were Williamson Park and Caton Road. The 3rd Battalion had a Watchers' Platoon under the Bishop of Lancaster, which manned the Ashton Memorial by day from June 1940 to July 1943 and by night until March 1942.

Some personal memories of being in the Home Guard are given on Lancaster's King's Own Royal Regiment website (kingsownmuseum. com). Harold Pye served in the Home Guard until February 1941 prior to serving in the RAF. He went to Bowerham Barracks for training which was carried out by soldiers who were just back from Dunkirk. He remembers making their own petrol bombs out of milk bottles and practising throwing them at High Cross near the Moor Hospital. He confirms that there was an observation post at the Memorial under the charge of a Captain English and they had to notify Barrow when planes flew over on their way to bomb Barrow shipyards. Captain English used to organise meat and potato pie suppers for the Guard and Harold used to take the pies up to the park and help give them out.

Iron Railings

In 1942 the *Lancaster Guardian* reported that the railings at Williamson Park, along with those on the Quernmore Road boundary, had been taken down as part of the war effort (30 October 1942). The writer surprisingly remarks that 'the effect is considered to be one of improvement', but worse is to follow. He went on to inform the reader that 'Someone with admirable courage has gone so far as to order the removal of that far from picturesque iron drinking fountain which used to flaunt its ultra Victorian facade upon the verge of the lovely lake. As an object d'art, it had long ago ceased to commend itself to anyone with an appreciation of the natural beauty of its surroundings, and its usefulness ceased when its mechanism broke down some years ago' (see section on the park in 1891).

Iron railings and other sources of iron were sent to steelworks in the belief that it would all be used for military purposes and so help with the war effort. Unfortunately the removal of the railings around the park made it much easier for instances of vandalism to occur, as reported in

Removal of railings 1940 (Lancaster City Museums)

the *Guardian* in 1945 from an anonymous letter writer calling himself 'A Ratepayer'. He stated that large amounts of timber were being removed by youths, beginning at the time of bonfires being held for VE Day and then VJ Day. 'Now, with the approach of November 5th, there are youths armed with axes and ropes on every school holiday and each week-end, who drag out huge logs and tree trunks over the wall into Wyresdale Road' (2 October 1945).

James Hodgson and the HMS *Audacity*

To finish this section on the wartime park, I would like to pay tribute to one of the young park gardeners who enlisted to join the Royal Navy and whose story was told in the *Lancaster Guardian* (30 January 1942). James Hodgson from Caton was born in 1912 and worked at Williamson Park from the age of 23 after working at Halton Park. He joined the Royal Navy in 1941 and was posted to HMS *Audacity*, an escort carrier (aircraft carrier), after completing his training. Sadly, the *Audacity* was sunk by a U-boat when acting as an escort to a convoy on 22 December 1941 and he was reported as missing, presumed dead. There were 225 survivors (see uboat.net/allies/merchants/ship/1233.htm for more information).

Lancaster's Natural History Museum

In 1931 the Corporation decided to set up Lancaster's own Natural History Museum within the Ashton Memorial. The *Lancashire Evening Post* reported that the Memorial would open to the public again in July 1932 following extensive alterations, so it seems likely that these were in connection with preparations for the new Museum. By September that year the Corporation had got round to appointing a sub-committee to procure cases and exhibits for the museum, one of whom was Councillor James Dowbiggin, who was also the curator at the Observatory. The Corporation's *Committee Minute Books* record many of the details discussed when setting up the museum.

It was decided that the museum would be on the first floor and that the Borough Surveyor and a Mr Bland should submit a scheme, beginning with a central octagonal case. A tender for £56 10s. from Waring and Gillow for supplying the case was accepted and subsequently the offer from Mr H Murray & Son of Carnforth to fill the show case with specimens of English birds at a cost of £42 was accepted.

Henry Murray established his taxidermy business in 1872 at 6–8 Scotland Road in Carnforth and was later joined by his son, Albert James, with the business continuing until Henry's retirement in 1961 (www.taxidermy4cash.com/murray.html). They were listed as saddlers in the 1911 census, which was probably their main source of income. They produced taxidermy specimens of the highest quality, including work for museums as well as private collectors. There is a fine collection of Murray taxidermy at Kendal Museum, including extinct species. The Murrays usually 'signed' their work, the cases having a large label on the back and a small one on the inside.

A large case of gulls presently in storage at Kendal Museum has a fine label on the back of the case, advertising the company as 'Naturalists and Specialists in Pictorial Taxidermy'. They advertise 'heads, horns, hoofs & fish mounted in the best manner'.

Included on a list of items they could make, macabre by today's standards, are 'foxs' pads mounted as paper knife, with bone, ebony or ivory blades, or as Ladies' Brooches'!

On Monday 8 May 1933, Henry Murray met with the sub-committee at the Ashton Memorial to discuss the provision of additional cases and specimens of birds. They agreed to obtain a quote for a case 5 feet 6 inches square and 6 feet in height, similar to the one already installed, and Mr Murray agreed to supply and mount specimens of gulls in the case for £48 17s.

The museum collection was added to again in 1936 when Mr Murray offered a collection of 'stuffed divers'. The committee agreed to purchase these for £57 10s., to include the mounting of the birds. They subsequently also ordered a suitable case for the collection from Waring and Gillow for the price of £52 10s.

In 1953 five items were placed on display in the Memorial's museum because the City Museum in town had no room for them. They were, however, not natural history specimens. They included a 'tree needle machine for doll making, an Eagle press proof machine, a very withered fire engine used in about 1730, an old harrow or plough, and an old churn' (*Lancaster Guardian* 1 May 1953).

It is known that there was livestock being kept in the Memorial during the 1960s, because when the structure was damaged by fire in 1962 the

Park Superintendent reported the kind assistance of a Mr T. Parkinson in temporarily housing the creatures. As reported by the *Guardian* on 20 July 1962 on the occasion of the fire, 'birds in cages in an aviary on the ground floor were taken to safety by firemen and Corporation employees ... The birds in the aviary, disturbed by the unaccustomed activity, set up a large screeching noise and were later removed to another part of the Park.'

The Corporation's *Committee Minute Books* record the theft of livestock from the park and Ashton Memorial in January 1963. The Park Superintendent was authorised to acquire a golden pheasant and the City Architect was asked to submit a report on the security arrangements at

An example of Henry Murray's stuffed birds from Kendal Museum

the Memorial. As the work to repair the damage to the Memorial caused by the fire had not been completed by this time, it seems likely that the building may not have been entirely secure.

Sadly, by 1976, the second-floor display of 750 stuffed birds had to be kept locked, the reason given being that there no supervision was available (*Lancaster Guardian* 15 October 1976). It is not clear what subsequently happened to these exhibits – it has not been established that any were sent to Kendal to be displayed in their museum.

The window cleaners of the Ashton Memorial

In 1952 the windows of the Ashton Memorial had their first proper clean, having previously been cleaned using hosepipes (*Lancaster Guardian* 12 September 1952). A local window-cleaning firm, Percy Bailey & Son, were given the job – they were also employed to clean the Town Hall windows and the windows of many other public buildings in the city. Percy, aged 57, was described by the *Guardian* as 'wiry-limbed and keen-eyed' and the job took him and four of his staff three days to complete. He explained that they used ordinary extension ladders and where these could not reach, they 'climbed out on the fabric in order to finish the job'. He stated that the most difficult to clean were the windows high in the dome under the copper roof and washing the long windows which led from the first floor to the circular room which housed the collection of birds. He reassuringly explained that every man in the team was insured!

Problems with structures and fires

The Ashton Memorial money pit

The unusual construction of the Memorial and cost-saving measures used at the time have resulted in ongoing maintenance problems over the decades, not helped by the severe fire-damage that occurred in 1962. As early as 1919, only ten years after construction was completed, the town's Building Surveyor submitted a report on the condition of the building and the Parks Committee felt the need to visit the park to inspect the 'Structure', 'particular attention being paid to the suggestions contained in the recent report'.

It therefore seems likely that some work was needed to bring it up to standard, although it was not until the following year that the Mayor and the Town Clerk had a meeting with Lord Ashton to discuss the state of the Memorial. It was probably with some relief that they reported back that Lord Ashton was willing to 'keep the Memorial in repair and for that purpose to put down a capital sum of money sufficient to permanently maintain the Memorial'. It is not clear from the Corporation Minute Books what further action was taken at that time; however, in 1922 the Committee was again seeking an interview with Lord Ashton 'with a view to placing before him the present financial position of the Williamson Park account'. Bearing in mind that this was only four years after the end of World War I, the Corporation was probably struggling for funds and anxious that Lord Ashton should keep his promise about the maintenance of the park and its buildings.

Nothing else is recorded in the Committee Minute Books until September 1930, only four months after the death of Lord Ashton, when the Mayor had an interview with Lord Peel (Lord Ashton's son-in-law). This resulted in Lady Ashton and Lady Peel (Lord Ashton's daughter, Ella), the beneficiaries of Lord Ashton's estate, agreeing to pay the cost of repairs required to the Ashton Memorial, estimated to be £2,100. They also agreed to set up an endowment fund of £6,000 for the maintenance of the Memorial, with the provision that the Corporation acknowledge them to be free from further liability.

Less than twenty years later, in 1947, the endowment fund was put to use when it was reported by the City Engineer that the Memorial would require around £1,000 worth of repairs. This was in addition to repairs to other park buildings: £400 for the Observatory, £300 for the bandstand and £500 for the Palm House. It is to be wondered what repairs were actually carried out, as in 1953 someone calling themselves 'Park Lover' wrote to the *Lancaster Guardian* (13 November 1953) complaining about the poor state of repair of the Memorial. He/she stated that it was advisable to 'make a dash through the main entrance, and above all not to look up at the crest above the door. The reason is they will be running the grave risk of having a piece of plaster falling upon them.' The writer went on to say that the ceiling over the entrance was in a dreadful state and had been for a few years!

Fire at the Ashton Memorial

On 18 July 1962 a large part of the Memorial was damaged by fire. The cupola at the very top of the building was completely destroyed and the wooden framework under the copper dome was damaged. The *Lancaster Guardian* (20 July 1962) reported that the blaze could be seen for miles around and that people flocked to the park to watch dozens of firemen fighting to control the flames. A turntable ladder was rushed to the scene, but when extended fully it fell far short of the blaze and the firemen had to use the internal staircase to access the fire. Water was pumped from the park lake and taken up hill to the fire by a shuttle service of fire engines. At the height of the fire the huge weathervane on the top of the Memorial crashed down and broke into burning fragments. Burning debris fell into the cavity between the copper covering of the dome and the oak framework and ignited a lining of felt and breeze concrete.

The fire started when two Lancaster Corporation plumbers were engaged in restoration work at the top of the Memorial where wooden pillars were being replaced. Scaffolding had been erected around the wooden cupola and when the fire started the two men dashed down to ground level to raise the alarm. One of them told a reporter 'The wood was very dry and the high wind must have caused it to catch fire very easily.' Plumbers were often the workmen who carried out lead dressing to structures, but why there would be anything to cause a spark is not clear.

In spite of the damage, it seems that members of the public were still allowed admission, as the Park Superintendent reported to the Committee that the admission fees had been reduced as a result of the fire. As seems to be usual, the wheels of the Council moved slowly, and it was not until the following spring that the contract for scaffolding at the Memorial was agreed, and the repair work was to take several years. A large waterproof cover was specially made at Storey Brothers White Cross mills and placed over a scaffold surround to protect the memorial from damage by weather.

In July 1964 it was estimated that the cost of repairs would be £15,000, some of which would be covered by insurance, and in September of that year a recommendation was made that the remainder of the coke breeze concrete should be removed and replaced with lightweight reinforced concrete, as it was having a corrosive effect on the steelwork of the structure. This was estimated to cost £4,000. The original cost-savings made at the time of construction now constituting a real problem.

> DID YOU KNOW?
>
> Breeze concrete is three parts fine coke, known as coke breeze, one part sand and one part Portland cement. It has poor fire-resistant qualities but it is cheap.

It was to be four years after the fire before the repair work was sufficiently advanced to allow the repair of the copper dome itself, and a quote of over £5,000 was accepted from Merseyside Plumbing Co. Ltd. Finally, in 1967, the repair work was completed for a total cost of £26,561, almost half of which was covered by insurance (*Lancaster Guardian* 24 November 1967).

Palm House fires

In March 1949 the Palm House was completely engulfed in flames, fanned by high winds. The *Lancaster Guardian* reported that hundreds of people watched from the steps of the 'Structure' and nearby paths as the firemen struggled to put out the blaze. One of the park rangers, a Mr R. Ellwood, raised the alarm and four fire engines attended, three of them from Lancaster. Water had to be pumped from the lake up the steep incline. Burning wood and falling glass increased the difficulty and damaged the hoses, but some of the firemen had to enter the building to remove a quantity of acetylene and paint stored inside.

Repair and renovation work on the Palm House had been in the process of being carried out in preparation for the new season. All the plants were destroyed.

Palm House fire damage in 1949 (Lancaster City Museums)

Another fire caused damage to the same building only two years later in September 1951. Workmen had been stripping off paint by burning with lamps, but it was suspected that a spark must have ignited the woodwork. The alarm was raised by a passing motorist who 'noticed puffs of smoke coming from the top of the building'. The *Lancaster Guardian* (28 September 1951) reported that the fire brigade's new engine had been able to travel at 50mph up East and Wyresdale roads! Luckily on this occasion the damage was limited to some timber beams at the top of the building.

1980s renovation work

Only 14 years after repair works to the dome following the fire, in 1981 the Memorial was reported to be in 'a worse and worse state of repair' (*Lancaster Guardian* 16 October 1981). Unfortunately, earlier attempts to renovate the structure had resulted in further problems when poor maintenance and wet weather in this exposed location led to water penetration and corrosion to the steel structure. This in turn caused loss of structural stability and the corner turrets became detached from the main structure.

The City Architect, Mr Charles Wilson, stated that if no repair works were carried out the progressive nature of the building defects would very quickly lead to a point where restoration was impractical. The estimated cost was to be £368,000. Protective hoardings had been erected and the public only had access to the ground floor. Eventually the Memorial had to be closed and boarded up. With the monument inaccessible, there remained one little oasis of calm in the Palm House. This stayed open, and on cold winter days was a place where parents could take the children for a picnic in the warmth, viewing the budgies and rabbits in the cages, amid the exotic rubber plants and spider plants.

Funding for repairs to the Memorial was an issue and it was thought that as the building was of national importance, there should be funding from a national level. Much of the funding was thus eventually obtained from the European Community Regional Development Fund, which contributed a grant of £735,000 towards the project. The renovation works included reconstruction of the external balconies on all levels using reinforced concrete and steel. The cupola was treated with liquid plastic paint to resist weathering and new metal-framed windows were installed.

Restoration of the
Memorial in progress
in 1986 (Lancaster City
Museums LM88 132/6)

Luckily the copper dome was still in good condition and the only repairs were to guttering and a new lightning conductor. The electrical wiring was replaced, and the marble floor restored (*Lancaster Guardian* 19 September 1986).

Upon completion of its £700,000 facelift the Memorial re-opened on 23 May 1987, with an admission charge of 20p to visit the first-floor viewing balcony. There was also a multi-projector and stereo sound presentation depicting the history of the Edwardians with an 80p entrance fee.

The following month the Palm House re-opened after its transformation into the Butterfly House at a cost of £150,000. The building had benefited from the addition of a cast-iron gallery which was apparently in the original plans but never built. The temperature was kept at 30°C and the impression was of a tropical garden, containing as it did trees such as banana and pineapple, with mainly exotic butterfly species from the Far East and South America. The Butterfly House contained its own hatchery from which the population of butterflies was replenished (*Lancaster Guardian* 26 June 1987).

A further development was a new external enclosure next to the Palm House for the breeding of endangered British species of butterflies under the supervision of entomologist Mr Bill Wheatley. The enclosure consisted of a netted timber structure covering an area planted up to represent a wild English country garden designed and planted by Mr Wheatley himself. The breeding programme was very successful and the enclosure contained 2,500 butterflies from 26 different species, some almost extinct. The public were not allowed into this enclosure in case the butterflies were trodden on or damaged, but there were plans to enlarge the enclosure and add viewing areas (undated newspaper clipping, Lancaster Library).

At the time, the Council had ambitious plans to develop the park into a type of Edwardian theme park. The new Pavilion shop and cafe had already been completed in conjunction with the conversion of the Palm House into the Butterfly House, and other improvements were planned to include restoring fountains, improving footpaths and some forestry work. The bandstand would be renewed and the waterfall reinstated. More controversial were plans to have 'Edwardian transport', a miniature railway, and a pub in Golgotha Lodge! A summer season of events would consist of steam engine rallies, carousels, a helter-skelter, and side-show games such as 'Aunt Sally' – where you had to knock the pipe out of the mouth of a wooden cut-out figure (*Lancaster Guardian* – no date, clipping from folder in Lancaster Library). Perhaps fortuitously, some of these planned developments did not take place. The lake was refurbished in 1999, together with the fountain, and the nearby waterfall was reinstated as part of the Heritage Lottery Fund Urban Parks Programme.

The Temple Shelter

The floodlighting of the Ashton Memorial

The floodlighting of the Ashton Memorial, which is now a fairly common occurrence, is something which has actually taken place for various occasions over the last century.

The first instance of this happening seems to have been in 1919. Britain celebrated peace on 19 July 1919 after the First World War officially ended with the signing of the Treaty of Versailles. A victory parade was held in Lancaster, as in many other places, and the celebrations included the floodlighting of the Ashton Memorial, as well as the lighting of beacon fires on the Lakeland peaks and on Ingleborough (*Lancaster Gazette*, 25 years ago column, 30 June 1944).

In 1931 the Memorial was illuminated in connection with the Michael Faraday centenary. The illumination was carried out by fixing four floodlight projectors fitted with 500-watt lamps to each of four 35-foot poles, using only 8 units of electricity per hour. The lighting occurred each evening between 8 and 11 pm for one week in September.

In 1935 the Memorial was floodlit as part of the events held in the town to

> ### DID YOU KNOW?
>
> The Michael Faraday Centenary was held to celebrate the passage of 100 years since the discovery of the principle of electromagnetic induction. It was organised by the Royal Institution and the Institution of Electrical Engineers, and included an exhibition at the Royal Albert Hall and a dedication plaque being placed on the floor of Westminster Abbey.

Experimental floodlighting of the Memorial in 1999
(Photo courtesy of Phil Leedal, Lee Engineering)

celebrate the Silver Jubilee of the reign of King George V, although this idea was initially rejected by the Council on the grounds of expense.

In 1952 floodlighting was for the Festival of Britain, at a cost of £400 for the summer season, and in 1953 floodlighting of the Memorial, as well as the Priory and the Town Hall, again took place for the coronation of Queen Elizabeth II. There had been some disagreement within the Council as to whether or not the city could afford to spend £250 to continue to floodlight the Memorial for the following summer, especially as it was felt that residents now took the lighting for granted. It was mentioned that this might be improved if the colours could be changed,

© Ian Greene

but again this would lead to more expense. However, it was agreed to carry on with the original scheme and letters to the local press in 1953 revealed that readers were pleased that the floodlighting would continue.

It was not until 1999 that the Memorial was lit in many colours. An innovative local firm, Lee Engineering, still based on Scotforth Road in Lancaster today, had the opportunity to trial a Danish state-of-the-art lighting system worth £100,000. This could reproduce any colour and project it onto buildings in a changing pattern operated by a remote programming system. The Council granted the firm permission to use the Ashton Memorial and the trial continued for a period of two weeks.

Nowadays the Memorial is regularly floodlit in different colours to highlightdifferent charities and causes, and is provided by a company called BCL Lighting Design. For example, in 2016 to celebrate St John's Hospice thirtieth anniversary the Memorial was floodlit in the Hospice's colours.

Beautiful photographs of the floodlit Memorial taken by various members of the public are regularly featured on Lancaster Past and Present's Facebook page.

'RAKU' sculpture

This mosaic sculpture is located about 100 metres up the main drive from the Quernmore Road entrance to the park on top of a small hill on the left. It was created in a collaborative project between staff and residents from the former Royal Albert Hospital in Lancaster and a creative art group called RAKU Sculptural Arts from Rawtenstall. The decision was taken to design and create a special sculpture in a place which many of the patients visited regularly to mark the impending closure of the hospital.

> **DID YOU KNOW?**
>
> The Royal Albert Hospital, originally called 'Royal Albert Asylum for idiots and imbeciles of the seven northern counties', opened in 1870 as an institution for the care and education of children with learning disabilities. Following new legislation in 1913, adults were also admitted. In the 1980s the patients were relocated into the community, and the hospital closed in 1996.

The patients were taken on local visits to favourite places and encouraged to draw their experiences of nature and the outside world – these firmed up to become trees, leaves, flowers, squirrels, the sea and fishing boats. The shapes in the sculpture were made from chicken wire which was then covered in several layers of concrete to achieve a smooth surface. Clay was used to make the tiles, which were glazed in colours chosen by the patients, the tiles then being fired in the artist's workshop. The tiles were broken up to make mosaic shapes which were then cemented onto the sculpture. The whole project was completed in six weeks and opened in 1992.

The sculpture was recently carefully restored by members of the Friends of Williamson Park.

The Raku Sculpture

Fenham Carr

In 1997 the park was extended to include the wooded area to the east known as Fenham Carr, following a grant from the Heritage Lottery Fund, resulting in a total area of 53.6 acres for the park. This land had been part of the estate of Lancaster Moor Hospital, previously known as the Lancaster County Lunatic Asylum, which finally closed its doors in 2000. At its height, in the 1940s, the hospital housed around 3,000 patients and employed almost 3,000 staff.

The first building belonging to the hospital opened in 1816 and the layout of the site can be seen on the 1891 Ordnance Survey map (see the earlier section concerning the park in 1891) adjacent to the park. A pleasant garden area and woodland walk would have been seen as beneficial activity for the patients. This map also shows the reservoir which was constructed in 1839 as water storage for the Asylum. Prior to this the only source of water was from a force-pump attached to a well below the foundations of the Asylum, worked by the manual labour of the patients! (*Lancaster Guardian* 25 December 1858). As the Asylum took more and more patients,

---

DID YOU KNOW?

Edmund Sharpe was an English architect, railway engineer, and sanitary reformer. He established an architectural practice in 1835 in Lancaster in his mother's house in Penny Street, taking on 15-year-old Edward Graham Paley as his pupil and moving to premises on Sun Street in the same year, 1838. During his career he designed many churches. In 1874, at the end of his life, he designed his last church, St Paul's at Scotforth.

architect Edmund Sharpe was asked to report on a possible solution to the ever-increasing demand for water. His suggestion was to pipe water from a spring on land called Knotts, near Stanley Farm in Quernmore, and to store this in a reservoir. This reservoir was used as the only water supply until the Asylum was connected to the mains sometime in the 1870s. After this date the reservoir was used as a supply of water for the fire brigade in the event of a fire at the Asylum.

'A Patient Drowned'

Unfortunately, the proximity of the reservoir in relation to the Asylum resulted in the drowning of a patient in 1887. Richard Cowban, aged 27, a labourer from Burnley, had been a patient there for four years. Dr Harding, one of the assistant medical officers, described him as 'always of a silly, flighty disposition'. Prior to his death he had made his escape whilst out in the grounds of the Asylum with a walking party, and was found by the reservoir, saying he had wanted to catch a swan which was there.

It was common practice for over one hundred patients to go for walks in the Asylum grounds with only five attendants, meaning each attendant had over 20 patients to keep an eye on. The patients were simply counted out and counted in again on their return, so anyone wandering off would not necessarily be noticed until then. Two weeks later he again escaped whilst out with another walking party but this time he could not be found, even after dragging the reservoir. His body was eventually recovered six days later by one of the attendants at the Asylum, John Waters, who had gone there to feed the swan, with no intention of searching for a body. He got into one of the boats and threw the grapple out which latched onto the body, which he brought to the side of the reservoir where he laid it. The body was fully dressed, with Richard's cap stuck in his belt and he had a pocket handkerchief tied over his head – apparently, he was in the habit of doing this.

Dr Cassidy, the medical superintendent at the Asylum, told the inquest that 'the remainder [of the patients] have always been sent to walk beyond the airing courts daily. Of these, the large majority are either imbecile or suffer from chronic mania, requiring very little supervision, and I consider that five attendants for 111 patients is ample'. The Deputy Coroner, Mr Whelon, was satisfied with this situation, saying that in his experience this was the first time that a patient had died in these circumstances. He was satisfied that every precaution had been taken to ensure the safety of the deceased and the other patients in the care of the institution (*Lancaster Gazette* 5 March 1887).

'Sad end of a Lancaster lad'

Only six years later, a 15-year-old boy named John Thomas Keegan was also drowned in the reservoir in Fenham Carr. A fortnight earlier he had been released from the Castle prison following a sentence of six weeks' hard labour for stealing pigeons. He met up with two friends, having promised to show them a throstle's nest in the grounds of the Asylum. One of the Asylum attendants ordered them out of the grounds, but Keegan persuaded the other boys to go back and climb over the railings around the reservoir, as he wanted to 'have an hour's sail for nothing'. He got into a canoe while his two younger friends got into one of the other two boats, but unfortunately he overbalanced and fell into the water. Richard Frankland of Henry Street, also aged 15, dived in to assist him but Keegan grabbed him by the leg. Frankland had to kick him off to save himself and consequently Keegan drowned. The two boys ran off and called at a nearby house to raise the alarm and his body was found by one of the Asylum doctors. On searching his body, the police inspector found in his pockets 'two pipes, a tobacco box and a piece of strap. There was no money'.

At the inquest the two boys who were with Keegan described climbing over the railings by using an iron hurdle which was leaning against the railings, but this must have been moved by someone later on, as the Coroner, Mr Holden, stated that he did not know how the boys had managed to climb over the 8-foot railings. Mr Holden described Keegan as 'a very wayward boy' and went on to say, 'He did now know but what his death might not be regarded as a happy one, as he would have met with many troubles if he had continued in the way he began.' At the end of the inquest the Coroner called Keegan's two friends back into the room and said he 'wanted them to think of the sad end of their playfellow, and of his untimely death, and keep it before their eyes and resolve in future to lead good lives, so that when their time came they might not fear death'. He then gave them one shilling each and hoped the jury would agree with him 'in expressing the hope that they would in future be good boys and grow to be good men' (*Lancaster Gazette* 20 May 1893).

Nowadays Fenham Carr is an important nature conservation area and provides a peaceful woodland walk consisting of mature trees including oak, holly, sweet chestnut, beech, pine and sycamore. There is also an orchard area and a wildflower meadow providing a varied habitat for birds, bats and insects. Foxes, hedgehogs, voles, deer and badgers have also been spotted there. Recently, as part of the RSPB birdwatch, fifteen species of birds were seen, including nuthatches, dunnocks, tree creepers, chaffinches, and song thrushes.

Fenham Carr bird feeder observation area

Views of the park

Modern developments in the park

Sundial

To celebrate the millennium, Lancaster City Council commissioned local artist, Ray Schofield, to design and cast a sundial in bronze to be placed on the site of the old bandstand, to the north of the Memorial. It is an analemmatic sundial, that is a sundial with hour points, rather than the usual hour lines, laid round an ellipse. These have a movable gnomon (the part that casts a shadow), and this is almost always a person. In the case of the bandstand sundial, each hour point is marked by a plaque with a design influenced by the local area. The plaques were designed with the help of pupils of Ripley St Thomas School in Lancaster.

The sundial was officially opened on 15 July 2000 and is reportedly one of the biggest in the country.

> ### DID YOU KNOW?
>
> Ray Schofield (1948–2004) lived at Sunderland Point towards the end of his life. His work includes paintings of the boats, landscape and buildings of the Point, but he was also known for his sculptures.

Williamson Park Sundial
Sundial plaques showing the Memorial and showing the Butterfly House

Mini Zoo and Butterfly House

In 2017 the Butterfly House was smartened up, with further restoration work to the roof and external painting, but also had a complete reorganisation of the internal layout and planting. A blue-tongued skink and a bearded dragon were added to the resident lizards, and over fifteen different species of tropical butterflies from around the world fly freely around the interior. The plants range from passion flowers, citrus and peace lilies, to shrimp plants and lantana. School groups are regular visitors and the Butterfly House can also host children's birthday parties.

The Mini Zoo and Mini Beast House to the rear of the Butterfly House now boast the additions in recent years of nine meerkats and two marmosets, in addition to rabbits and guinea pigs. The meerkats arrived in 2016 from Leeds Tropical World Zoo, and the marmosets in 2018 from Monkey World in Dorset, which is a monkey sanctuary and rescue centre. There is also an aviary in which the birds nest and fly freely around the enclosure and a mini beast 'cave' containing clawed frogs, blind fish and giant snails among other creatures. The Mini Zoo also gives children the opportunity to attend 'Meet the Keeper' days during school holidays.

Palm House interior today

The Friends of Williamson Park

The Friends of Williamson Park group is a registered charity which supports the City Council in maintaining and developing the gardens and natural areas, the historic features, play areas and buildings. The aim is to improve accessibility and promote the use of the park for everyone. The group has been running in its present form since 2011, although a group of volunteers worked in the park prior to this. Past projects have included creating a new woodland play area, creating a beautiful 'Friends Garden' in one of the dells, and restoring the Cascade. The Cascade feature was re-discovered when the group were clearing rhododendron bushes next to the southern end of the lake and was in a sorry state – the pump was broken, the cobbles were loose and vegetation had grown over the rock face. The Cascade was successfully restored and switched back on in April 2017.

The Friends have encouraged more wildlife to visit the Fenham Carr area through activities such as setting up 150 bird boxes and creating a feeding station. Currently they are in the process of organising the renovation of the Raku sculpture which has suffered some loss of its mosaic tiles since it was first constructed. They hold regular book sales in the Ashton Memorial to help raise funds to carry out their work. You can learn more about the Friends at lancaster.gov.uk/sites/williamson-park/ friends-of-the-park.

Cycling events

The park is regularly used for cycling events and has a long history of being used by cycling clubs. In June 2019 the first ever Lancaster Grand Prix race began and finished at Williamson Park as part of the National Road Series – British Cycling's flagship event.

The 100-mile course featured seven laps of a circuit running through the Forest of Bowland Area of Outstanding Natural Beauty, and boasted a top-class field of over 100 riders from the national elite cycling teams. During the day a free festival of family fun events and displays took place in the park. It was planned to hold this event again in June 2020 coinciding again with a family fun day including live music and stalls promoting healthy lifestyles, but had to be cancelled due to COVID-19.

Postcard of girl cyclist *c*.1900 standing outside park gates (Lancaster City Museums LANLM.1996.45.135)

The popularity of the park as a destination for cyclists was illustrated by the fact that the Lancaster section of the Cyclists' Touring Club requested facilities for the parking of cycles at the park in 1937. It was agreed that facilities would be provided at the entrance gates, but that notices would be erected to the effect that the Corporation would accept no liability for the safety of cycles parked there. During the 1960s the park was regularly closed to the public for the closed-circuit cycle racing meetings of the Lune Racing Cycling Club.

Plays and concerts

Since 1987 Lancaster's own Dukes Theatre has put on a promenade performance during the summer months using the natural scenery of the park as a backdrop, and now more than half a million people have enjoyed the Play in the Park. The very first performance was *A Midsummer Night's Dream* in which Andy Serkis, who later achieved film fame as Gollum

The 2021 park production of Grimm Tales.
(Photo © Grant Archer / The Dukes)

in *Lord of the Rings,* appeared as Lysander at the age of 23. Andy is now Honorary Patron at the Dukes. The 2016 promenade production of *The Hobbit* won Best Show for Children and Young People at the UK Theatre Awards.

For 2019 the Dukes took a break from producing a play in the park, and the planned 2020 production of Alice in Wonderland had to be cancelled due to COVID-19. The theatre also hosts outdoor cinema screenings in the park during the summer, known as Sunset Screenings.

Other plays are regularly performed by travelling theatre groups and these take place in the open-air theatre area known as The Dell. In 2019 Illyria outdoor theatre group performed *Frankenstein* and in 2018 it was Shakespeare's *The Merchant of Venice*.

Another innovation is the Highest Point Festival, held for the first time in 2018 and repeated in 2019, featuring various music acts over several stages. It lasts for three days over a weekend in May and culminates with the Big Family Day Out on the Sunday, including interactive theatre, DJs, storytelling, arts and crafts, face painting and free entry to the Butterfly House and Mini Zoo. The 2019 festival was attended by over 15,000 people and included acts such as Sister Sledge, The Zutons and Grandmaster Flash. It received rave reviews, not least for its family-friendly atmosphere.

Highest Point Festival, © Robin Zahler

Children's play areas

There are two children's play areas in the park, one for under eights at the north side of the Memorial near the cafe, and one for over eights at the western side of the Memorial, at the bottom of the hill. These were fully refurbished, re-opening in spring 2016, and won the Lancashire Environmental Fund Best Practice Award for a play area. The City Council provided the bulk of the funding, but the Friends group secured the rest from the Lancashire Environmental Fund.

One of the Park's play
areas.

Park Run

Williamson Park is still helping to keep the townspeople fit and healthy. Upwards of 250 people of all ages and abilities run around it every Saturday morning on the 5km Park Run, which began in January 2016 (http://www.parkrun.org.uk/lancaster/)

Part of the 'Friends Garden', showing one of the quarry faces
One of the dells converted into an outdoor auditorium

Future Plans

There are big plans for the future development of the park, including replacing the present Pavilion cafe and shop building with a new £4 million pound wedding and conference centre, which would include a larger cafe, a retail area and an education suite. The Ashton Memorial already hosts over 100 wedding ceremonies a year – Lancaster's Member of Parliament since 2015, Cat Smith, got married in the park in 2016, one of the guests being Jeremy Corbyn, the then leader of the Labour party. The new centre would enable wedding parties to also take place within the setting of the park (*Lancaster Guardian* 19 April 2018).

At the present time there is also a proposal to create a treetop trail or 'Lost Castle' attraction similar to the one in the grounds of Lowther Castle within Fenham Carr at the eastern end of the park. This adventure play area would aim to enhance and utilise the natural assets of the woodland area. It is hoped that such developments would make the park into a top visitor attraction in the area, providing extra funds for improvements in other areas of Fenham Carr, specifically to increase biodiversity (lancaster.gov.uk/parks-and-open-spaces).

History has demonstrated that there have been many plans and innovative ideas for how to use the park, some of these have resulted in exciting new developments, others never got off the ground. We can anticipate that this will continue into the future.

However, the park is now a thriving focus for the inhabitants of Lancaster and visitors alike. On a summer's day it is usually alive with families enjoying the pleasures of this beautiful place, created through the efforts, vision and labours of our Lancastrian predecessors.

Interior of Ashton Memorial showing ceiling paintings by George Murray

Memories of the Park

Williamson Park feels like an extension of our back garden, really, we and our small children absolutely love it! We're up there in all weathers, it's always amazing, different every time. Can't believe how lucky we are to have it on our doorstep, we never tire of it.

***

My favourite time in the park is the quiet early morning – no distractions from listening to birdsong, seeing the seasonal changes in the plants and trees, and the clear views across Morecambe Bay from the top of the Ashton Memorial steps.

***

As a kid, growing up near Williamson Park meant it was a place to meet up, play and explore with friends. There were more bushes at the sides of the monument back then and we used to hide in them, as a game with each other or to escape the park warden, whose sole job appeared to consist of stopping kids from having fun climbing trees, rock faces and nicking into the Butterfly House, which we referred to as the 'Hot House'. You couldn't stay in too long though, it was like a sauna back then, red hot!

More recently, it's a place I love to use for exercising with clients and small groups. I now appreciate all the beauty the park has to offer, which I took for granted as a child.

All the green spaces, well maintained garden areas, trees, paths and even the cafe, would attract me to visit. But, the Ashton Memorial, standing high above the city of Lancaster, is a fantastic sight to see from a distance. Once you are closer, though, you can really appreciate all of its splendour. The steps just invite you to climb them and the building itself is peppered with details you can miss if you don't look close enough. It's only in recent years I've noticed a train embossed into the face of the building, for example.

And then there's the views across the city and Morecambe Bay, which always create lasting memories for me. On a clear day you can see all the way to the mountains of the Lake District. Simply stunning.

***

I visit the park early three times a week meeting friends
For circuit training exercise
Up and down the memorial steps
Seeing Morecambe Bay and the mountains
Doing sits ups gazing at the gargoyles, the dome and the architecture
We see the seasons pass
The trees changing colour
The beautifully kept park
The friendly dog walkers
We do this in all weathers
In the rain we're under the eaves
Looking up at the Lego patterns
When it's dry we're fully outside
The stars in the winter
The sun in the summer
All chatting away
What a way to start the day!

Thank you, James Williamson

***

Williamson Park: it's my go-to place. For solace, meditation, for a walk or a coffee, for the daffs and the azaleas, the trees and butterflies. It's my go-to place to admire horizons, meet friends, enjoy conversations. It's my go-to place for quiet contemplation.

***

Born and raised within a stone's throw of the green memorial dome. Now living at the other side of the world. It's not my family or friends that bring me back to the evergreen park yearly, it's the childhood of wonderful memories created there.

***

Williamson Park means my happy youth. I was born on Park Road in 1963 (a few minutes away from Williamson Park). As a young child we walked around the park and fed the ducks most weekends. My teens were spent with friends playing in the park (1970s). Life was so much fun and we always felt safe there. I remember the drinking fountain near the pond where we all drank from. We spent hours playing hide and seek, riding our bikes and roller skating. We never realised at the time how lucky we were as we just took it for granted, as it was just our playground. My boyfriend in 1978 (who is my husband today) also lived near the park and we used to meet in the park. In the 80s we took our own children to the park at weekends and we still often go there for a walk around 50 years later. All my memories are good apart from one when I was about 12 and someone came rushing out of the bushes covered in wasps. I am still scared of wasps.

Postscript

History by its very nature never comes to an end. Life can take unexpected turns, and 'normality' can suddenly change. At the present time, life for the people of Lancaster, and indeed the rest of the world, has changed in ways which could never have been imagined only a few months ago. At the beginning of 2020, it was reported in the news that a previously unknown virus was spreading from country to country, and it wasn't long before the word 'pandemic' started to become part of our everyday conversation. The spread of COVID-19 (a coronavirus) across the world resulted in millions of deaths and unprecedented changes to all aspects of life. In March 2020 the government introduced instructions that all people apart from those working in essential occupations should remain indoors as far as possible, only going out to buy essential supplies such as food and medicines, to exercise, or in specified urgent situations. This became known as 'lockdown' and there have been two further lockdowns since to date.

Although the rules varied in the different lockdowns, they all allowed individuals or members of a household to go outside once a day for the purpose of exercise, with the proviso that a 2-metre 'social distance' was maintained from other people. The roads of Lancaster, as elsewhere, were much quieter, non-essential shops, pubs and cafes were all closed, all those who could work from home were requested to, schools and nurseries faced various degrees of closure, and holidays were more or less impossible within the rules.

During this time the use of the park changed significantly. The cafe, shop, zoo and Butterfly House were all closed, and the Memorial was locked up. The usual crowds of locals and visitors who would in normal years flock in great numbers to the park to enjoy its beauty, the activities it has to offer, and a tasty snack from the Pavilion Café, were much reduced. However, the park was still a haven for all ages, a favourite place for many Lancaster residents, enjoying their once-a-day outdoor allowance, whether alone or with family or friends. This use increased hugely during the periods between lockdowns, although moving along its paths and trails required greater awareness of others, with frequent stops or changes in direction as people attempted to maintain the safe distance. Children who previously used the park to run around and burn off energy or explore in the trees were now supervised and told to stay close to their parents.

At the time of writing, in the midst of the third lockdown, a huge vaccination programme is underway, which it is hoped will allow us to begin to shape a new normal in the next few months. Although there remain many uncertainties, as has always been the case throughout its history, Williamson Park has proved itself to be a truly invaluable resource, much beloved by the people of the city and far beyond.

References and further reading

Ashworth, Sue, *The Lino King* (Lancaster City Museums: Lancaster, 1989).

Caton Village Exhibition Committee, *Caton – Past and Present* (Castle Press: Lancaster, 1979).

Fleury, Cross, *Time-Honoured Lancaster* (Eaton and Bulfield: Lancaster, 1891).

Gardner, Norman, 'The Coulston Family's Part in the Catholic Revival in Lancaster', *Contrebis*, vol. 23 (1998).

Gooderson, Philip J., *Lord Linoleum* (Keele University Press: Keele, 1996).

Harker, John, 'British Interments at Lancaster Moor', *Journal of British Archaeological Association (JBAA)*, vol. 21 (1865).

Harker, John, 'On further discoveries of British Remains at Lancaster Moor', *JBAA*, vol. 28 (1872).

Harker, John, 'British Interments at Lancaster', *JBAA*, vol. 33 (1877).

Hird, Frank, *Lancashire Stories Illustrated, Volume 1* (T. C. and E. C. Jack: London and Edinburgh, *c.*1900).

Hudson, Phil, *Quarrying and Extractive Industries* in *Rural Industries of the Lune Valley*, edited by Michael Winstanley (Lancaster University: Lancaster, 2000).

Janes, Derek, *Lancaster* (Dalesman Books: Whitehaven, 1980).

Johnson, Thomas, *An Illustrated Booklet about the Williamson Park, Lancaster* (T. Johnson: Blackburn, *c.*1896).

Johnson, Thomas, *A Pictorial Handbook to the Valley of the Lune* (T. Johnson: Blackburn, 1885).

Kemp, Edward, *How to Lay Out a Garden* (Bradbury and Evans: London, 1858).

Lancaster and District Heritage Group, *St George's Works Mill, A landmark ofLancaster's Industrial Past* (LDHG: Lancaster, 2018).

Lancaster and District Heritage Group, *The Ladies in the Life of Lord Ashton* (LDHG: Lancaster, 2018).

Lancaster and District Heritage Group, *The Last Will and Testaments of James Williamson Snr and James Williamson Jnr, Lord Ashton* (LDHG: Lancaster, 2018).

Owen, Richard, *Report on the State of Lancaster* (W. Clowes and Son: London, 1846).

Peel, Edgar & Southern, Pat, *The Trials of the Lancashire Witches* (David & Charles: Newton Abbot, 1969).

Price, James, 'Industry and Changes in its Location in 19th century Lancaster', *Contrebis*, vol. 20 (1995).

Sailor, Dan, *The County Hanging Town* (Challenge Publishing: Lancaster, 1994).

Waddell, J. D., *Williamson Park* (Lancaster City Council: Lancaster, *c.*1956).

Wade, Peter, 'In Search of Lancaster's Lost Observatory', *Contrebis*, vol. 33 (2010).

Whalley, Mike, *The Grandest Monument in England* in *Aspects of Lancaster*, edited by Sue Wilson (Wharncliffe Books: Barnsley, 2002).

White, Andrew, *The Buildings of Georgian Lancaster* (Lancaster University Centre for North-West Regional Studies: Lancaster, 1992).

White, Andrew, 'The Folly to End all Follies?' *The Follies Journal*, vol. 6 (2006).

White, Andrew, 'Who was Mr McLean of Castle Donington?' *Contrebis*, vol. 26 (2001).

White, Andrew and Winstanley, Michael, *Victorian Terraced Houses in Lancaster* (Centre for Northwest Regional Studies: Lancaster, 1996).

Winstanley, Michael, 'The Town Transformed, 1815–1914' in *A History of Lancaster 1193–1993*, edited by Andrew White (Ryburn Publishing: Keele, 1993).

Online resources

British Library Newspapers for *Lancaster Gazette*, accessed free with a library card through the following link by selecting 'British Library Newspapers 1730–1950': https://www.lancashire.gov.uk/libraries-and-archives/libraries/digital-library/?page=5

'Find My Past' for access to newspaper articles and censuses, accessed via a subscription.

Friends of Williamson Park https://www.lancaster.gov.uk/sites/williamson-park/friends-of-the-park

Historic England entry for Williamson Park https://historicengland.org.uk/listing/the-list/list-entry/1000942

Jim Jarrat's Follies website. *The Ashton Memorial*. 2004. www.jimjarratt.co.uk/follies/page42.html

Journal of Antiquities website. *Golgotha Lodge, Williamson Park*. 2018. https://thejournalofantiquities.com/2018/07/26/golgotha-lodge-williamson-park-lancaster-lancashire/

Lancaster Civic Society. *Lancaster's Canalside Mills*. 2014. https://lancastercivicsociety.files.wordpress.com/2014/06/canalside-mills-c.docx

Memorial Drinking Fountains website. *Williamson Park Drinking Fountain*. 2018. https://memorialdrinkingfountains.wordpress.com/2018/04/22/williamson-park-drinking-fountain/

St George-in-the-East Church website. *St Matthew Pell Street 1848–1891*. www.stgitehistory.org.uk/stmatthewpellstreet.html

Lancashire Archive references

Committee Minute Books of Lancaster Corporation 1855–1874. Ref: MBLA acc11602/7. Deeds relating to Williamson Park and others. Ref: DDX909 acc11506/box3.

Ledger and cash book for Ashton Memorial and Palm House. Ref: MBLA acc11602/25-26.

Letter from James Williamson to Mayor and other documents. List of documents given to solicitors, Oglethorpe, Sturton & Gillibrand on 9 June 1988. Ref: DDX909 acc9109/box111

Letters of Thomas Storey to WGJ1 with circulars and draft answers 1862. Ref: DDQ 7/35/23.

Community History Section, Lancaster Library

Plan of the Stone Quarries. 1814, PL1/50. Plan of Lancaster Moor. 1820, PL1/51.

Corporation Minute Books 1895–1967